Context@HTL

COMPANION

1 bis 5

Gemeinsam besser lernen

Contents

Contents

1 Grammar

1.1 Personal and possessive pronouns

1 I have a message from <u>Anita Richards</u>. **She** wants to see you later.

2 Did you see <u>Brendan Smith</u> yesterday? – Yes, I saw **him** in the shopping centre.

3 <u>My friend</u> and I discussed <u>the problem</u>. **We** decided what to do about **it**.

4 Is this <u>the marketing manager's</u> laptop? – That's right. It's **her** laptop.

Wenn wir eine bereits erwähnte Person oder Sache im Laufe eines Textes oder Gesprächs nochmals erwähnen wollen, benutzen wir oft Pronomen *(pronouns)*, anstatt die Person / Sache immer wieder beim Namen zu nennen.

So sehen die Pronomen im Englischen aus:

Subjekt		Objekt		Possessiv	
I	*ich*	me	*mich / mir*	my	*mein / e*
you	*du*	you	*dich / dir, euch, Ihnen*	your	*dein / e, euer / eure, Ihr / e*
he	*er*	him	*ihn / ihm*	his	*sein / e*
she	*sie*	her	*sie / ihr*	her	*ihr / e*
it	*es*	it	*es / ihm*	its	*sein / e*
we	*wir*	us	*uns*	our	*unser / e*
they	*sie*	them	*sie / ihnen*	their	*ihre / e*

 ▶ Vorsicht beim Übersetzen von Sie / sie ins Englische: *you, she / her* oder *they / them?*

▶ Vorsicht beim Übersetzen von Ihr / ihr ins Englische: *you, her, your* oder *their?*

1.2 The sentence

Aufbau des Satzes: *word order* (Satzstellung)

1 My father works in **a supermarket**.
2 He goes **there every morning**.
3 He **usually** doesn't order new products.
4 He **is** always very helpful.
5 She does her homework **carefully**.

- **Orts- und Zeitangaben** stehen in der Regel am Satzende. [1, 2] Kommen sowohl Orts- als auch Zeitangaben vor, steht die Zeitangabe nach der Ortsangabe. [2]
- **Häufigkeitsangaben** (wie oft?) wie *always, usually, often* ... stehen immer vor dem Hauptverb. [3]
- Die Formen *am / is / are* stehen jedoch vor einer Häufigkeitsangabe. [4]
- **Adverbien der Art und Weise** stehen nach dem Verb (und auch nach dem Objekt zum Verb). [5]

Aufforderungen aussprechen: *imperatives*

positive Aufforderung	negative Aufforderung
Buy some bread on your way home, please.	**Do not park** here. **Don't forget** to post the letters, please.

- Wie im Deutschen wird der Imperativ verwendet, um jemanden aufzufordern, etwas zu tun bzw. nicht zu tun.
- In positiven Sätzen entspricht der Imperativ dem Infinitiv ohne *to*.
- In negativen Sätzen stellen wir *do not* (schriftlich oder förmlich) oder *don't* (alltäglich) vor den Infinitiv.

Fragen stellen: *asking questions*

Aussage	Entscheidungsfrage	wh-Frage
1 Ruby is from London.	Is Ruby from London?	Where is Ruby from?
2 Lucy has seen the Diwali lights.	Has Lucy seen the Diwali lights?	What has Lucy seen?
3 Lucy likes Leicester.	Does Lucy like Leicester?	What does Lucy like?
4 Lucy should listen to Ruby.	Shouldn't Lucy listen do Ruby?	Who should Lucy listen to?
5 Lucy and Ruby are going shopping tomorrow.	Are Lucy and Ruby going shopping tomorrow?	When are Lucy and Ruby going shopping?

- Steht im Aussagesatz ein Hilfs- oder Modalverb (z. B. *be, have, should*), bilden wir Entscheidungsfragen (*yes / no-questions*), indem wir dieses Hilfsverb an den Satzanfang stellen. [1, 2, 4, 5]
- Bei Aussagesätzen ohne Hilfsverb bildet man Fragen, indem man *do / does* an den Satzanfang bzw. vor das Subjekt stellt. [3]
- Möchten wir bestimmte Informationen erfragen, benötigen wir ein Fragewort (*Who? When? Where? Why? What? How long? Whose?*). Dieses kommt an den Satzanfang. Das Hilfsverb bzw. *do / does* steht vor dem Subjekt.
- Um verneinte Fragen zu bilden, ergänzen wir *not / n't* nach dem Hilfsverb. [4]

Substantive mit Relativsätzen näher bestimmen: *relative clauses with relative pronouns; contact clauses*

1 Relativsätze mit Relativpronomen *(relative clauses with relative pronouns)*

1 Nick Hardy is somebody **who / that** just loves to complain.
2 This is the canoe **which / that** is too small for a camper.
3 These guides tried to help **people whose** tents were damaged in the storm.
4 This is the **minibus whose** door fell off on the way to the campsite.
5 My friend Mona, **who** has just come back from her trip to Nepal, loves nothing more than travelling.

- Relativsätze werden benutzt, um ein Nomen durch zusätzliche Informationen näher zu bestimmen.
- Für **Personen** benutzt man das Relativpronomen *who* bzw. *that* [1], für **Sachen** *which* bzw. *that*. [2]
- Um **Besitz** oder **Zugehörigkeit** anzuzeigen, gebraucht man *whose* unmittelbar vor dem Nomen bei Personen und Sachen. [3, 4]
- Ist der Relativsatz notwendig, um das Bezugswort eindeutig zu identifizieren, spricht man von einem *defining clause*. In diesem Fall wird vor dem Relativpronomen **kein Beistrich** gesetzt [1–4].
- Bei **non-defining clauses**, also Relativsätzen, die zusätzliche Informationen zum Bezugswort enthalten, welche nicht unbedingt notwendig sind, setzt man vor dem Relativpronomen einen **Beistrich**. Geht der Hauptsatz nach dem Relativsatz weiter, muss auch am Ende des Relativsatzes ein Beistrich gesetzt werden. [5]

2 Relativsätze ohne Relativpronomen *(contact clauses)*

1 The van **(which / that)** we normally use wasn't available.
2 The van **that / which** came to get the tourists was an hour late.

- Steht das **Relativpronomen** für das **Objekt** des Relativsatzes, dann kann man es **weglassen**. Solche Relativsätze heißen **contact clauses**. [1]
- Wenn das **Relativpronomen Subjekt** des Relativsatzes ist, darf es **nicht wegfallen**. [2]

Bedingungen formulieren: *if-sentences*

- Wollen wir die Folgen einer Handlung darstellen, z. B. um jemandem einen Rat zu erteilen oder jemanden vor etwas zu warnen, verwenden wir oft einen *if*-Satz (Bedingungssatz).
- Ein *if*-Satz besteht aus zwei Teilen: dem ***if*-Teil** und dem ***Hauptteil***. Der *if*-Teil drückt eine Bedingung aus, der Hauptteil eine Folge.
- Steht der *if*-Teil zuerst, wird er durch ein Komma vom Hauptteil abgetrennt. Steht der Hauptteil zuerst, steht kein Komma.

 ▸ Im *if*-Teil steht niemals would! (*If*-Sätze sind würde-los.)

If-sentence type 0

If-Sätze vom Typ 0 folgen diesem Muster:

If-clause	main clause
If + simple present	simple present

1 If you **push** the red button, the machine **stops** working.
2 The machine **runs** faster if / when you **push** the green button.

- In *if*-Sätzen vom Typ 0 beschreiben wir Folgen, die unter der beschriebenen Voraussetzung voraussichtlich **immer** eintreten werden. (*Jedes Mal, wenn ..., passiert X.*)
- Üblicherweise kann man in Typ 0 *if*-Sätzen das *if* auch durch **when** ersetzen. [2]

If-sentences type 1

If-Sätze vom Typ 1 folgen diesem Muster:

If-clause	main clause
if + simple present	will + infinitive

1 **If** I **see** him, I **will tell** him that.
2 I **will enjoy** my stay in Malta **if** the people there **are** nice.

- In *if*-Sätzen vom Typ 1 sagen wir, was unter bestimmten Voraussetzungen geschieht bzw. was wahrscheinlich geschehen wird.

If-sentences type 2

If-Sätze vom Typ 2 folgen diesem Muster:

If-clause	main clause
if + simple past	would / could / might + infinitive

1 **If** I **were** you, I **would not do** that again.
2 I **would** really **go** to Malta **if** my parents **allowed** me to.
3 **If** I **were** an alien, I **would be able** to fly.

- *If*-Sätze vom Typ 2 drücken Situationen aus, die unwahrscheinlich oder sogar unmöglich sind: Was wäre, wenn ... [3]

 ▸ Statt der *simple past*-Form was steht im *if*-clause oft, vor allem im formellen Sprachgebrauch, *were*.

*if-*sentences type 3

*If-*Sätze vom Typ 3 folgen diesem Muster:

*If-*clause	main clause
if + past perfect	would / could / might + have + past participle

1. If I **had known** that, I **would** never **have done** that.
2. She **could have gone** out with her friends if she **hadn't been** at the pizza service.
3. You **might have got** better marks if you **had worked** harder.

■ In *if-*Sätzen vom Typ 3 beschreiben wir Situationen, die gar nicht mehr passieren können, da sie bereits vergangen sind: „Was wäre gewesen, wenn …" . Häufig drücken wir damit **Bedauern** darüber aus, dass etwas nicht geschehen ist.

1.3 Tenses

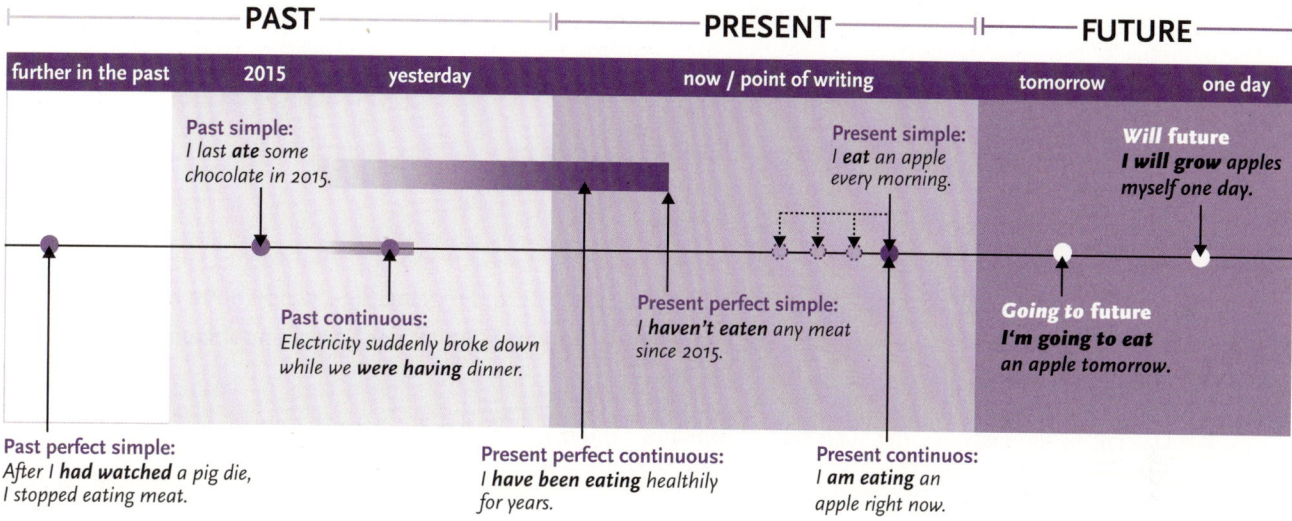

Beschreiben, was gewöhnlich geschieht: *present simple* (einfache Gegenwart)

Aussage	Verneinung	Frage
The Galloways **live** in Cork. Jane Galloway often **plays** basketball.	Kevin **does not / doesn't like** dancing.	**Does** Tessa Galloway **work**?

■ Wir verwenden das *simple present* für gleichbleibende Zustände (= was immer so ist) und regelmäßige, wiederholte Handlungen (= was wir immer / oft so machen – z. B. Tagesablauf), aber auch für *plot summaries* (Zusammenfassungen).

■ Außer in der **dritten Person Singular** (*he / she / it*) hat das *simple present* die gleiche Form wie der **Infinitiv**.

■ Bei *he / she / it* wird ein **-s** an die Grundform angehängt: *play – plays, say – says*.

⚠ ► Beachten Sie die **Sonderformen**: *go – goes, miss – misses, watch – watches, wash – washes, fly – flies*.

■ Wenn es kein Hilfsverb im Satz gibt, werden **Verneinungen** und **Fragen** mit *do / does* gebildet.

■ Die folgenden **Signalwörter** stehen oft mit dem *simple present*:

always • never • often • rarely • (hardly) ever • sometimes • occasionally • now and then • generally • normally • regularly • usually • every day / week / month / … • on Mondays / …

Beschreiben, was zurzeit geschieht: *present progressive* (Verlaufsform der Gegenwart)

Aussage	Verneinung	Frage
Jane and Kevin **are watching** TV at the moment.	Tessa **is not / isn't doing** the shopping now.	**Are** the Galloways **working** in the garden at present?

- Wir benutzen das *present progressive* für vorübergehende oder **im Moment des Sprechens** ablaufende Handlungen und Situationen.
- Das *present progressive* bilden wir mit *am / is / are* und der *-ing*-Form des Verbs.
- **Verneinungen** werden mit *not* bzw. *n't* gebildet.
- **Fragen** werden gebildet, indem *am / is / are* und das Subjekt vertauscht werden.
- Folgende Verben, die **Zustände oder Gefühle** ausdrücken, werden üblicherweise **nicht** im *present progressive* gebraucht:

  be • believe • dislike • hate • know • like • love • mean • notice • see • seem • want • wish

- Die folgenden **Signalwörter** stehen oft mit dem *present progressive*:

  at present • at the moment • currently • now

Present simple – present progressive

1 People are often angry and react in a very unfriendly way when nobody helps them.
2 The friendly clerk at the store is smiling to the customer.
3 We are interviewing people on the streets tomorrow.

- Wir verwenden das *present simple* für **gleich bleibende Zustände** und **regelmäßige, wiederholte Handlungen**. [1]
- Wir benutzen das *present progressive* für **vorübergehende** oder **im Moment des Sprechens ablaufende** Handlungen und Situationen. [2]

⚠️ ▸ Das *present progressive* steht auch häufig für **Pläne**, für die schon **konkrete zeitliche Abmachungen** getroffen worden sind. Meist weist dann eine Zeitangabe auf den Zukunftsbezug hin. [3]

Über die Vergangenheit berichten: *past simple*

Aussage	Verneinung	Frage
Kathleen **wanted** fabulous clothes. She **bought** some expensive shoes on the internet yesterday.	Unfortunately, she **did not / didn't have** enough money to pay.	**Did** Kathleen **try** to steal a designer blouse last Friday?

- Die einfache Vergangenheit (*simple past*) verwenden wir, wenn wir von Vergangenem berichten, also z. B. vom letzten Urlaub, vom Vortag, aus der Kindheit usw.
- Bei **regelmäßigen Verben** wird die einfache Vergangenheit gebildet, indem man **-ed** an die Grundform hängt. **Unregelmäßige** Verben bilden eine eigene Form (siehe S. 27 f., *Irregular verbs*).
- **Fragen** werden mit *did* und dem Infinitiv des Verbs gebildet.
- In **Verneinungen** steht *did not* (Kurzform: *didn't*) und der Infinitiv.
- Folgende **Signalwörter** stehen häufig mit dem *past simple*:

  yesterday • the day before yesterday • the other day (neulich) • two / three days / weeks / months / years ago • last night / week / month / year • last January / spring / Christmas • in 2008 / … • at that time • in those days

- Die Vergangenheitsformen von *be* sind *was* und *were*. Verneinung: *was not* (*wasn't*) und *were not* (*weren't*).
- **Zeitangaben** stehen am Satzanfang oder -ende. Dabei steht das Wort *ago* immer am Ende der Zeitbestimmung:

  two days ago / 42 years ago / seven minutes ago / …

Konkrete Situationen in der Vergangenheit beschreiben: *past progressive*

Aussage	Verneinung	Frage
Kathleen **was walking** down Liffey Road when she found a new boutique. Some people **were looking at** clothes while a woman **was trying on** a coat.	Mrs Connors **was not / wasn't looking** when Kathleen took the blouse.	**Was** Kathleen's father **watching** TV when Mrs Connors phoned?

- Mit dem *past progressive* wird eine Handlung beschrieben, die zu einem bestimmten Zeitpunkt in der Vergangenheit im Verlauf war.
- Es wird vor allem dann benutzt, um zu beschreiben, dass eine Handlung im Gange war, als (plötzlich) eine zweite Handlung (*simple past*) geschah.
- Es wird oft nach *while* (= während) benutzt.
- Das *past progressive* wird aus *was / were* und der *-ing*-Form des Verbs gebildet.
- Die **Verneinung** wird mit *not* bzw. *-n't* gebildet. In **Fragen** werden *was / were* und das Subjekt vertauscht.
- Folgende Verben stehen normalerweise **nicht** im *past progressive*:

  be • believe • dislike • hate • know • like • love • mean • notice • see • seem • want • wish

Über die Vergangenheit sprechen: *simple past – past progressive*

1 Ali and his Austrian business partner **met** for dinner at a restaurant in town.
2 They **were walking** home again when they **saw** the poster.

- Das *simple past* verwenden wir, wenn wir von etwas berichten, das zu einem **bestimmten Zeitpunkt** oder in einem **bestimmten Zeitraum** in der Vergangenheit geschehen ist. [1]
- Mit dem *past progressive* wird eine Handlung beschrieben, die **zu einem bestimmten Zeitpunkt im Gange war**. Es wird vor allem dann benutzt, wenn eine Handlung im Verlauf war, als eine zweite Handlung (*simple past*) geschah. [2]

Handlungen und Vorgänge mit Bezug zu Vergangenheit und Gegenwart beschreiben: *present perfect*

Aussage	Verneinung	Frage
Young people **have lost** interest in traditional hobbies. The internet **has made** a big difference. Your posters **have** just **arrived**, Mark.	Printers send me posters that **they have not / haven't** folded yet.	How many posters **have** you **collected** so far, Mark?

- Das *present perfect* wird für Handlungen und Vorgänge verwendet, die irgendwann einmal – oder noch nie – stattgefunden haben, ohne Angabe des Zeitpunkts. Erwähnt man den Zeitpunkt (ist dieser also auch wichtig), steht das *simple past*.
- Wir benutzen das *present perfect* auch, um auszudrücken, dass etwas in der Vergangenheit begonnen hat und bis in die Gegenwart andauert, also noch nicht abgeschlossen ist.
- Das *present perfect* drückt oft auch aus, dass die Handlung in der Vergangenheit (konkrete, wahrnehmbare) Auswirkungen auf die Gegenwart hat.
- Das *present perfect* bilden wir mit *have / has* und dem Partizip Perfekt (3. Form des Verbs). (Die Formen unregelmäßiger Verben finden Sie in Appendix D, *Irregular verbs*.)

- Bei der **Verneinung** steht *not* oder *never* zwischen *have / has* und dem Verb.
- Bei **Fragen** ohne Fragewort steht *have / has* am Satzanfang.
- Das *present perfect* wird häufig mit folgenden **Signalwörtern** gebraucht:

> *ever • never • all day • still (not) • (not) yet • just • lately • recently • up till now*

- *Since* und *for* (= seit) stehen im Englischen mit dem *present perfect*. *Since* steht mit einem **Zeitpunkt** (z. B. *since January*), *for* mit der Angabe einer **Zeitdauer** (z. B. *for three weeks*)

Present perfect oder *past simple*?

> **1** I **have never been** to Vietnam.
> **2** **Last year,** we **went** to Vietnam for our summer holiday.

- Für Handlungen oder Vorgänge, die irgendwann einmal – oder auch noch nie – stattgefunden haben, verwenden wir das *present perfect* [1]. Der Zeitpunkt, also wann das stattgefunden hat, spielt dabei keine wesentliche Rolle.
- Erwähnt man den **Zeitpunkt** einer vergangenen Handlung (ist dieser also wichtig), steht das *simple past* [2]. Es beschreibt, was zu einem bestimmten Zeitpunkt (oder in einem bestimmten Zeitraum) in der Vergangenheit geschehen ist.

Ausdrücken, dass etwas seit längerer Zeit im Gange ist: *present perfect progressive*

Aussage	Verneinung	Frage
Mark **has been collecting** posters since he was 12.	He **has not / hasn't been buying** posters from India for very long.	How long **have** you **been doing** your hobby, Mark?

- Wir benutzen das *present perfect progressive*, um auszudrücken, dass eine Handlung oder ein Vorgang schon länger andauert.
- Das *present perfect progressive* steht oft mit *since* + **Zeitpunkt** oder *for* + **Zeitdauer**.
- Wir bilden das *present perfect progressive* mit *has / have been* und der *-ing*-Form des Verbs.
- Bei **Verneinungen** steht *not* bzw. *-n't* nach *has / have*.
- In **Fragen** werden *has / have* und das Subjekt vertauscht.

Über die Vergangenheit mit Gegenwartsbezug sprechen:
present perfect simple – present perfect progressive

> **1** Rick **has changed** so much over the past months.
> **2** We **have been trying** to reach him all day, but we haven't succeeded yet.

- Wir benutzen das *present perfect simple*, um auszudrücken, dass etwas in der Vergangenheit begonnen hat und **unmittelbare Auswirkungen auf die Gegenwart hat**. [1]
- Wir benutzen das *present perfect progressive*, um auszudrücken, dass eine Handlung oder ein Vorgang **schon länger andauert und noch nicht abgeschlossen ist**. [2]

Die Vorvergangenheit ausdrücken: *past perfect*

1 Before Rita went to Plymouth, she **had seen** all the sights of Exeter.
2 After he **had spent** a year in England, Lukas was happy to see his friends at home again.
3 Lukas **had not / hadn't slept** at all the night before he left for England.

- Das *past perfect* bildet man mit *had* und dem *past participle* des Verbs. [1, 2]
- Bei **Verneinungen** steht *not* bzw. *-n't* zwischen *had* und dem *past participle*. [3]
- Mit dem *past perfect* drückt man aus, dass eine Handlung vor einer anderen in der Vergangenheit stattgefunden hat.
- Das *past perfect* wird häufig in Sätzen mit folgenden Konjunktionen verwendet:

after • before

Über die Zukunft reden: *future forms*

1 *Going to* future

Aussage	Verneinung	Frage
The authorities **are going to introduce** speed limits. Look at those clouds. It **is / It's going to snow.**	I **am / I'm not going to do** anything, Alan.	**Are** you **going to make** footballers wear crash helmets?

- Das Futur mit *going to* verwenden wir für Pläne und Absichten, also z. B. um auszudrücken, was wir gerade vorhaben. [1]
- Mit *going to* kann man auch sagen, dass etwas höchstwahrscheinlich geschehen wird. [2]
- Das *going to*-Futur wird mit *am / is / are going to* + Infinitiv gebildet.
- Bei **Verneinungen** steht *not* hinter *am / is / are*.
- **Fragen** bilden wir, indem wir *am / is / are* und das Subjekt vertauschen.

2 *Will* future

Aussage	Verneinung	Frage
High-speed sports for thrills **will lead** to some accidents. I hope the authorities **will introduce** speed limits. You've missed your bus? Don't worry. I **will / I'll drive** you home.	People **will not / won't go** onto the slopes at all.	**Will** safety rules **spoil** the fun?

- Das *will future* verwenden wir für ...
  - Vorhersagen,
  - Vermutungen über die Zukunft,
  - Hoffnungen,
  - spontane Entscheidungen,
  - Versprechen.
- Das *will future* bilden wir mit *will* und dem Infinitiv ohne *to*. Die Form bleibt in allen Personen gleich.
- **Verneinungen** bilden wir, indem *not* hinter *will* eingefügt wird.

  ⚠ ▸ Oft steht für *will not* die Kurzform *won't*.

- In **Fragen** werden *will* und das Subjekt vertauscht.

3 *Present progressive* und *simple present* mit Zukunftsbedeutung

> **1** Ben and Sarah **are staying** with us **next week.**
> **2** The TV technician **is coming after 8 o'clock tomorrow evening.**
> **3** Tom's train **leaves** for Linz **at 8:28 tomorrow morning.**
> **4** Don't forget that the main film **starts at 8 o'clock on Saturdays.**

- Wenn für Pläne schon konkrete zeitliche Abmachungen getroffen worden sind, steht häufig das *present progressive*. Meist weist dann eine Zeitangabe auf den Zukunftsbezug hin. [1, 2]
- Das *present simple* verwendet man für Fahrpläne, Programme usw. [3, 4]

1.4 The passive

> **1** The roads around here **are used** a lot less now.
> **2** Passengers for Tokyo **were put on** another flight.
> **3** The BA flight **has been delayed** for two hours.
> **4** Refreshments **will be served** at 11 o'clock.
> **5** It's a scheme that **can be** easily **set up** *by* councils.
> **6** The roads **are not used** as much.
> **7** **Are** cars **being used** less?

- Das Passiv verwenden wir, wenn wir auf eine unpersönliche Art und Weise über Fakten, Vorgänge usw. berichten wollen. Wir heben damit nicht den Verursacher (also z. B. die handelnde Person), sondern den Vorgang hervor. Oft wird der Verursacher nicht genannt oder ist gar nicht bekannt. [1–4, 6, 7]
- Soll der Verursacher einer Handlung genannt werden, steht im Passivsatz *by* (= von, durch). [5]
- Das Passiv wird mit einer Form von *be* und der 3. Form des Verbs gebildet. [1–4]
- Kommt ein Hilfsverb im Satz vor, steht dieses vor der Form von *be*. [5]
- **Verneinte Sätze** bilden wir, indem wir *not / never* vor das Partizip stellen. [6]
- **Fragen** im Passiv werden gebildet, indem man die Form von *be* und das Subjekt vertauscht. [7]

Verwendungsmöglichkeiten des Passivs: *by-agent* und *impersonal passive*

1 *By-agent*

> **1** Many of our town centres have already been destroyed **by out-of-town shopping.**
> **2** I'm talking about goods that are delivered **by van.**
> **3** Credit cards are used **by many customers** because they make shopping easier.
> **4** The prices were even lower than I'd been told.
> **5** British factory outlets can't be compared to those in the States.

- Wenn man in einem Passivsatz erwähnen will, von wem etwas getan wird oder wodurch etwas geschieht, fügt man diese Information mit der Präposition *by* an ⚠ ▸ nicht *from* . [1–3]
- Ist der Verursacher einer Handlung nicht wichtig, kann der *by-agent* weggelassen werden. [4, 5]

2 Unpersönliches Passiv (*impersonal passive*)

> **1** **It is said / thought that** consumers are spending more on luxuries now.
> **2** Hundreds of years ago, **it was said / thought that** the world was flat.

- Mit Verben des Sagens und Denkens bildet man das unpersönliche Passiv (*impersonal passive*):
  It is / was + Passivform + *that*
- Das *impersonal passive* wird vor allem in neutralen, objektiven Texten wie Zeitungsberichten verwendet, wenn die Informationsquelle nicht genannt werden soll.

1.5 Modal auxiliary verbs

Englisch	Deutsch	Ersatzverb	Beispiel
can	können (Bitte)		**Can** I speak to Jan, please?
could / may	könnten / dürfen (höfliche Bitte)		**Could** you give me her number? **May** I have her number, please?
can / could	können / konnten (Fähigkeit)	be able to	I **can** understand some German.
can / could	können / konnten, dürfen (Erlaubnis)	be allowed to	You **can** / You're **allowed to** use your mobile with a microphone while driving.
must	müssen (Verpflichtung)	have to	You **must** / **have to** call Sam at once.
must not may not	nicht dürfen (Verbot)	not be allowed to	You **mustn't** use your mobile in hospitals.
need to	brauchen (Notwendigkeit)		I **need to** get his number.
needn't	nicht müssen, nicht brauchen (freie Wahl)	not have to	I **needn't** / **don't have to** charge my mobile very often.
may	möglicherweise tun		Some people **may** buy third generation mobiles.
might / could	könnten (Möglichkeit)		Some people **might** use them.
should	sollten (Empfehlung)		You **should** phone Sam before he goes to work.
ought to	sollen (Empfehlung)		You **ought to** have been there! It was great.

⚠ ▶ Hilfsverben können nicht ohne Vollverb stehen: *Gesa kann Spanisch.* = *Gesa can* **speak** *Spanish.*

- Mit *can* – oder dem Ersatzverb *be able to* – drücken wir eine **Fähigkeit** aus. *Can* – oder das Ersatzverb *be allowed to* – steht auch, wenn man von einer **Erlaubnis** spricht.
- Die Vergangenheitsform von *can* lautet *could* oder *was / were able to*.
- In der Regel verwenden wir für das deutsche *müssen* das Hilfsverb *have to*. Geht es jedoch um eine strengere **Verpflichtung**, gebrauchen wir *must*.

⚠ ▶ Da *must* keine **Vergangenheits- oder Futurformen** hat, braucht man für diese Zeitformen das Ersatzverb **have to**: *had to / did not have to* oder *will (not) have to*.

- **Verbote** drücken wir mit *must not / mustn't* aus. Will man sagen, dass für etwas **keine Verpflichtung** oder **keine Notwendigkeit** besteht, braucht man *do not / don't have to* oder *need not / needn't*.
- Möchten wir ausdrücken, dass etwas möglich oder wahrscheinlich ist, benutzen wir *may*. Ist etwas weniger wahrscheinlich, brauchen wir *might* oder *could*.
- *May, might, would* oder *should* können sich auch auf Zukünftiges beziehen: *'We may never know.'*
- **Empfehlungen** oder **Ratschläge** drücken wir mit *should (not)* oder (etwas förmlicher) *ought (not) to* aus.

1.6 Adjectives and adverbs

Dinge und Handlungen beschreiben: *adjectives and adverbs*

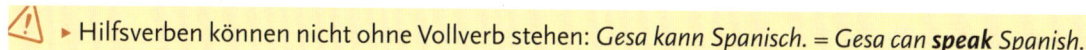

1 A good film needs **convincing** actors.
2 Joëlle Baker acts **convincingly**. / Joëlle Baker is a **really** convincing actor.
3 Last year Joëlle Baker made three films. She works very **hard**.
4 The main song in her new film sounds so **good**.

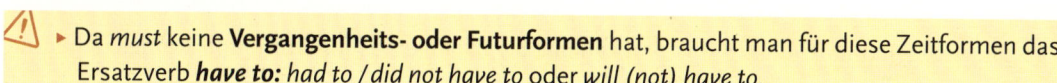

- Adjektive bestimmen meist ein Nomen näher. [1]
- Mit Adverbien beschreibt man, wie etwas geschieht. Man kann damit auch Adjektive näher beschreiben. [2]

- In der Regel werden Adverbien durch Anhängen von *-ly* an das Adjektiv gebildet: *final – finally*.
- Es gibt einige unregelmäßige Adverbien. Die wichtigsten sind *good – well* und *hard – hard*. [3]
- Auf bestimmte Verben folgt ein **Adjektiv, kein Adverb**. [4]

> *to be • to taste • to look • to sound • to feel*

Vergleiche ausdrücken: *comparison of adjectives*

Im Englischen gibt es zwei Arten der Steigerung: eine mit *-er / -est* und eine mit *more / most*.
Auf welche Art ein Adjektiv gesteigert wird, hängt vor allem davon ab, wie viele Silben es hat.

	Adjektiv	Komparativ	Superlativ
Einsilbige Adjektive	long big	long**er** big**ger**	(the) long**est** (the) big**gest**
Zweisilbige Adjektive, die auf -y enden	lucky	luck**ier**	(the) luck**iest**
Adjektive mit zwei und mehr Silben	famous horrible	**more** famous **more** horrible	(the) **most** famous (the) **most** horrible
Unregelmäßige Adjektive	good bad much / many little far	better worse more less farther / further	(the) best (the) worst most least farthest / furthest

1.7 Nouns

Countable and uncountable nouns

> 1 Chop **an onion**, **two tomatoes** and **four carrots** into small **pieces**.
> 2 To make the sauce, you need **flour**, **milk** and **salt**.
> 3 Mix in **three cups of milk** and **two pinches of salt**.

- Nomen wie *onions*, *tomatoes* und *carrots* sind zählbar. Sie haben eine Pluralform und können daher mit Zahlwörtern oder dem unbestimmten Artikel (*a / an*) stehen. [1]
- Wörter wie *flour*, *milk* und *salt* dagegen sind nicht zählbar. Sie bilden keine Pluralform und können daher nicht mit Zahlwörtern oder *a / an* verwendet werden. [2]
- Wenn wir bestimmte Mengen bezeichnen, d.h. nicht zählbare Nomen zählbar machen wollen, müssen Wendungen wie *three cups of …*, *two pinches of…* , *a piece / bit / packet of …* etc. verwendet werden. [3]

Irregular plurals

> 1 **Wolves** don't need **knives** to cut **potatoes** – because they rather eat meat!
> 2 The **children** are watching two cats running after a couple of **mice** in the yard.
> 3 As the saying goes, there **are** plenty more **fish** in the sea.
> 4 They found a pile of **clothes** on abandoned **premises** on the **outskirts** of the city.
> 5 My **family** always **gather** for birthdays./ My **family** always **gathers** for birthdays.
> 6 The **police were** first to arrive at the accident.

- Endet ein Nomen auf *-f(e)*, bildet es üblicherweise den Plural mit *-ves*. Bei Wörtern auf *-o* kommt im Plural -es dazu [1]: *wolf – wolves; knife – knives; potato – potatoes*.

- Manche Nomen, z. B. *child* oder *mouse*, bilden unregelmäßige Pluralformen, die einfach gelernt werden müssen [2]. Weitere wichtige Beispiele:

  > *child – children • foot – feet • goose – geese • louse – lice • man – men •*
  > *mouse – mice • tooth – teeth • woman – women*

- Andere Wörter ändern ihre Form im Plural nicht [3]. Dazu gehören:

  > *aircraft • deer • fish • moose • series • species • sheep*

- Einige Nomen haben keine Singularform – sie stehen immer im Plural [4].
- Daneben gibt es *collective nouns* wie z. B. *family, government, team*, die sowohl mit einem Verb im Singular als auch einem Verb im Plural verwendet werden können [5].
- *Police* steht immer mit einem Verb im Plural [6].

1.8 Quantifiers

Some, any und davon abgeleitete Wörter

> 1 Add **some salt** to the potatoes.
> 2 Can you give me **some salt**, please?
> 3 Can I get you **some more coffee**, John?
> 4 If you don't have **any butter**, use cooking oil.
> 5 Is there **any milk** in the fridge?
> 6 **Somebody** saw Mike and Jody go into the changing rooms.

- *Some* und *any* bezeichnen oft eine unbestimmte Menge oder Zahl.
- Vor nicht zählbaren Substantiven wie *butter* oder *music* bedeutet *some* „etwas". Oft steht für *some* und *any* jedoch keine direkte Entsprechung im Deutschen.
- *Some* wird vor allem in bejahten **Aussagesätzen** [1], **Bitten** [2] und **Angeboten** [3] verwendet.
- *Any* steht meist in **verneinten Aussagesätzen** [4] und in **Fragen** [5].
- Für die von *some* und *any* abgeleiteten Wörter gelten dieselben Regeln. [6]

Much, many, a lot of und *plenty of*

> 1 We don't need **many eggs**.
> 2 How **many tomatoes** do we need?
> 3 Don't add too **much salt**, please.
> 4 How **much butter** do we need?
> 5 I bought **a lot of / lots of potatoes** today.
> 6 Joshua used **a lot of / lots of lemon juice**.
> 7 Julie added **too much salt** to the sauce.
> 8 There are **plenty of onions** in the kitchen.

- *Many* wird mit **zählbaren** Nomen gebraucht [1, 2], **much** mit nicht zählbaren [3, 4].
- *Much* und *many* stehen überwiegend in **verneinten Sätzen** [1, 3] und **Fragen** [2, 4].
- In bejahten Sätzen steht *a lot of* oder *lots of*, sowohl mit **zählbaren** [5] als auch mit **nicht zählbaren** [6] Nomen.

  > ⚠ ▸ In bejahten Sätzen nach *as, how, so, too* [7] und *very* steht *much / many*.

- *Plenty of* („eine Menge", sehr viel / viele) steht sowohl mit **zählbaren** [8] als auch mit **nicht zählbaren** Nomen.

(A) little, (a) few

1 Add **a little water** if necessary. *(ein wenig)*
2 You need **a few carrots**, too. *(ein paar)*
3 Chris has **little interest** in Jody now. *(nur wenig)*
4 **Few people** really believed Jody's story. *(nur wenige)*
5 Only **a few** people came to the party where they only served **a little** fruit.

■ Wir verwenden *(a) little* mit **nicht zählbaren** [1, 3] und *(a) few* with **zählbaren** [2, 4] Nomen.

1.9 Reported speech

1 "Some parents <u>are damaging</u> their children by forcing them to compete in professional sport."

→ Hanna Foster **said** that some parents **were damaging** their children by forcing them to compete in professional sport.

2 "The media <u>turned me</u> into a big tennis star overnight."

→ Ms Foster **said** that the media **had turned** her into a big tennis star overnight.

3 "If anything, the situation <u>has become</u> even worse."

→ She **felt** that, if anything, the situation **had become** even worse.

4 "These children <u>will pay</u> dearly for their lost childhood."

→ Hanna **added** that **those** children **would pay** dearly for their lost childhood.

5 "It <u>cannot</u> be right to rob children of their right to grow up normally."

→ Ms Foster **told her audience** that it **could not be** right to rob children of their right to grow up normally.

■ In der indirekten Rede *(reported speech)* wird berichtet, was jemand gesagt, geschrieben oder gedacht hat.

■ Die indirekte Rede wird gewöhnlich mithilfe eines **einleitenden Verbs** *(reporting verb)* wiedergegeben. Die häufigsten *reporting verbs* sind *to say* [1, 2] und *to tell* [5]. Es empfiehlt sich allerdings, in der Verwendung dieser Verben zu variieren [3, 4]. Weitere geläufige *reporting verbs* sind:

to add • to advise • to agree • to announce • to answer • to ask • to beg • to claim • to command • to declare • to inquire • to instruct • to maintain • to mention • to plead • to point out • to promise • to suggest

■ Steht dieses *reporting verb* im *past simple* – z. B. *said* [1, 2], *felt* [3], *mentioned, pointed out, added* [4], *told* + Objekt [5] –, verschieben sich die Zeitformen des Verbs in der indirekten Rede wie folgt:

direkte Rede	indirekte Rede
present tense	past tense [1]
past tense	past perfect [2]
present perfect	past perfect [3]
will	would [4]

■ Modale Hilfsverben ändern sich auf ähnliche Weise:

direkte Rede	indirekte Rede
can	could [5]
may	might
must	had to

- **Zeit- und Ortsangaben** ändern sich dem Sinn des Satzes entsprechend, wie im Deutschen:

direkte Rede	indirekte Rede (einige Wochen später berichtet)
today	that day
yesterday	the day before / the previous day
the day before yesterday	two days before / previously
tomorrow	the next / following day
the day after tomorrow	two days later
this week / month / year / Easter / ...	that week / month / year / Easter / ...
next week / month / ...	the following week / month / ...
last year / August / ...	the year / August / ... before, the previous year / August / ...
now	then
at this time	at that time
these days	those days
here	there

- Ebenso ändern sich **Pronomen** dem Sinn des Satzes bzw. der Sicht des Berichtenden entsprechend. [2]
- Ist in der direkten Frage **kein Fragewort** vorhanden (Entscheidungsfrage), wird die indirekte Frage mit *if* oder *whether* (= ob) eingeleitet. [1, 2]

Aufforderungen, Ratschläge und Bitten anderer wiedergeben:
reported orders, advice, requests

1 "Don't disturb me again – I have a lot to do."
  → He **told** me **not to disturb** him again; he had a lot to do.
2 "Enter your name before you start."
  → She **advised** us **to enter** our names before we started.
3 "Could you help me with this translation, please."
  → She **asked** me **to help** her with the translation.

- Aufforderungen, Ratschläge und Bitten werden in der indirekten Rede meist durch einen *to*-Infinitiv wiedergegeben: **einleitendes Verb** im *simple past* + *(not) to* + Infinitiv. [1–3]
- Die häufigsten einleitenden Verben für solche Sätze sind:

  to advise • to ask • to invite • to offer • to order • to refuse • to remind • to tell • to warn

- **Zeit- und Ortsangaben** sowie **Pronomen** ändern sich dem Sinn des Satzes bzw. der Sicht des Berichtenden entsprechend, wie bei Aussagen in der indirekten Rede.

1.10   Participle constructions

Verwendungsmöglichkeiten des Partizip Präsens und des Partizip Perfekt –
using the present participle and the past participle

Das Partizip Präsens ist die *-ing* Form des Verbs.
Das Partizip Perfekt ist der Infinitiv + *-ed*. Einige Partizipien haben eine unregelmäßige Form, z. B. *made*
(siehe S. 27 f., *Irregular verbs*).

1 Our boss is always prepared to try out **promising** ideas.
2 The **damaged** goods will have to be replaced.
3 The people **working** in my department are not very friendly.
4 'Imagine' is a ballad **written** by John Lennon.
5 Norma Brown sits in her office all day long **typing** letters, reports and emails.
6 **Using** only the best ingredients in its dishes, the restaurant became known for its outstanding quality.
7 **Funded** by the government, the company is financially secure.

- Beide Partizipien werden oft **zur näheren Bestimmung eines Nomens** verwendet und haben dort dieselbe Funktion wie ein Adjektiv. [Präsens: 1, Perfekt: 2]
- Beide Partizipien **können einen Relativsatz ersetzen**. [Präsens: 3, Perfekt: 4]
  *The people **working** in my department = The people **who / that work** in my department*
  *A ballad **written** by John Lennon = A ballad **which was written** by John Lennon*
- Das Partizip Präsens (die *-ing* Form) steht auch **nach bestimmten Verben** der Ruhe und Bewegung, [5] z. B.:

  to sit • to lie • to go • to come • to stay

  ⚠ ▸ *She sits typing* heißt: *Sie sitzt da und tippt.*

- Beide Partizipien werden verwendet, um zwei Sätze kürzer in einem gemeinsamen Satz auszudrücken; vor allem, wenn zwischen beiden Sätzen ein gewisser kausaler Zusammenhang besteht (oder ein solcher angedeutet werden soll). [Präsens: 6, Perfekt: 7]
  *The restaurant became known for its outstanding quality **because** it only used the best ingredients. [6]*
  *The company is financially secure **because** it is funded by the government. [7]*

Unterscheidungsmöglichkeiten zwischen dem Partizip Präsens und dem Partizip Perfekt –
deciding when to use the present participle or the past participle

1 'Kit's Wilderness' is a story **involving** people of all age groups.
2 **Leaving** the hotel in a hurry, they almost forgot their suitcases.
3 **Designed** exclusively for the school, the new playground was the perfect way to use the space.
4 **Caused** by cars and other vehicles, the pollution in the city had reached dangerous levels.

- Das Partizip Präsens hat eine **aktive Bedeutung** und steht häufig mit einem Akkusativobjekt. [1, 2]
  *'Kit's Wilderness' is a story that **involves** people ... / They **left** the hotel in a hurry.*
- Das Partizip Perfekt hat eine passive Bedeutung und steht häufig mit einer Präposition. [3, 4]
  *Designed for the school, the new playground ... = The new playground **was designed for** the school.*
  *Caused by cars, the pollution ... = The pollution **is caused by** cars.*

1.11 Infinitive or -*ing* form?

Verben mit Infinitiv oder -*ing* Form? – *verb + to-infinitive or verb + -ing form?*

1 **I want to open** an account, please.
2 Joanna **enjoyed playing** with her new mobile.
3 Tom **prefers to go / going** into town by bus.
4 **I would like to speak** to you after the lesson, Laurie.
5 In the 1960s, employers **started paying / to pay** their workers monthly.
6 Look! It's **starting to snow**.
7 Please **stop to buy** some bread.

■ Manche Verben stehen **immer mit dem *to*-Infinitiv** [1]. Die häufigsten von ihnen sind:

to afford • to agree • to choose • to dare • to decide • to expect • to forget • to hope • to intend • to learn • to mean (beabsichtigen) • to offer • to promise • to refuse • to seem • to threaten (drohen) • to want • to wish

■ Manche Verben stehen **immer mit der -*ing* Form** [2]. Die häufigsten von ihnen sind:

to admit (zugeben) • to avoid (vermeiden) • to consider (bedenken) • to deny • to dislike • to enjoy • to finish • to imagine • to keep • to mind (etwas dagegen haben) • to miss (versäumen, verpassen) • to practise • to suggest

■ Die Verben *to like, to live, to hate* und *to prefer* [3] können mit beiden Formen stehen. Folgen sie auf *would (would hate, would like* usw.), kann nur der *to*-Infinitiv stehen, nicht die -*ing* Form. [4]
■ Die Verben *to begin, to continue, to intend, to plan* und *to start* können ebenfalls mit beiden Formen stehen [5]. Wenn sie hingegen in einer Verlaufsform stehen, ist nur der *to*-Infinitiv möglich. [6]
■ Bei einigen Verben gibt es Bedeutungsunterschiede, je nachdem, ob sie mit *to*-Infinitiv oder mit -*ing* Form stehen [7]. Die wichtigsten von ihnen sind *to remember, to stop* und *to try.*

– Do you **remember** meet**ing** John for the first time?	*sich erinnern*
– Please **remember to** give John my best wishes.	*daran denken*
– Lots of people have **stopped** smok**ing** recently.	*aufhören*
– I must **stop to** get some petrol.	*unterbrechen, anhalten*
– Why don't **you** try think**ing** for once?	*probieren*
– **I tried to** repair the car, but I couldn't.	*versuchen*

1.12 The gerund

1 **Working** in an office can often be strenuous, especially when the telephone keeps ringing all the time.
2 Despite **working** overtime, Peter decided to go to the cinema and watch a good film.
3 How serious is the risk of **losing** your job?
4 We're tired of **waiting**.
5 He had really been looking forward to **working** for the company.
6 He could not help **laughing** at the expression on her face when she saw his new office.

■ Das Gerundium kann die **Rolle eines Nomens** übernehmen. So kann es z. B. als Subjekt eines Satzes verwendet werden. [1]
■ Ein Verb nach einer **Präposition** *(after, before, by, despite, for, of, without* usw.) steht immer als Gerundium, also in der -*ing* Form. [2–5]
■ Die **Präposition** kann entweder **alleine** stehen [2] oder mit einem **Nomen** [3], einem **Adjektiv** [4] oder einem **Verb** [5] verbunden sein.

2   Vocabulary

2.1 Collocations

Collocations are combinations of words that are often used together in English, e.g. *make a plan, a heavy smoker.*

- It is a good idea to learn collocations like vocabulary.
- A table like the one below will help you to remember them more easily. Make three sentences with the collocations from the table that are true for you personally. Then try to make similar collocation tables for other words (e. g. challenge …)

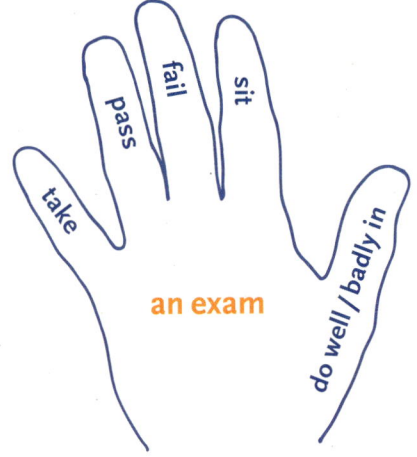

gain		_____
have	experience	in doing sth.
learn from		_____
go through the		of (doing) sth.

2.2 False friends

The following English and German words sound and look similar, but have different meanings. Be careful not to confuse them.

English	German		German	English
actual	*eigentlich*	≠	*aktuell*	current
announcement	*Ankündigung*	≠	*Annonce*	advertisement
become	*werden*	≠	*bekommen*	get
brave	*tapfer*	≠	*brav*	well behaved, good
chef	*Küchenchef*In	≠	*Chef*In	boss
direction	*Richtung*	≠	*Direktion*	principal's office
engaged	*verlobt; eingestellt; beschäftigt*	≠	*engagiert*	comitted
eventually	*schlussendlich, schließlich*	≠	*eventuell*	perhaps
fabric	*Material, Stoff*	≠	*Fabrik*	factory
form	*Formular*	≠	*Formel*	formula
gift	*Geschenk*	≠	*Gift*	poison
gymnasium	*Turn-, Sporthalle*	≠	*Gymnasium*	grammar school
handy	*praktisch*	≠	*Handy*	mobile (phone) (BE), cell phone (AE)
map	*(Stadt-)Plan, Landkarte*	≠	*Mappe*	folder
public	*Öffentlichkeit; öffentlich*	≠	*Publikum*	audience
prospect	*Aussicht auf etw., Perspektive*	≠	*Prospekt, Broschüre*	brochure
sensible	*vernünftig*	≠	*sensibel*	sensitive
spend	*ausgeben; verbringen*	≠	*spenden*	donate
sympathetic	*mitfühlend*	≠	*sympathisch*	likeable
wink	*zwinkern*	≠	*winken*	wave

2.3 Confusables

Many English words sound similar (e.g. *advice* and *advise*) or even exactly the same as others (e.g. *break* and *brake*), so it is easy to mix them up.

1 I need your advice. Please advise me on this.
2 He also came along although he didn't feel well.
3 You will break the brake if you keep pulling it like that.
4 A cool dessert tastes delicious in the hot sandy desert.
5 How does it affect you? What effect does it have on you?
6 I'd like to lie in the sun and lay my hand on her arm; really, I'm not lying.
7 Don't lose this loose button.
8 The show is called *Live a Happy Life* and it's going out live to the nation.
9 I may have won the prize, but I've certainly paid the price for it.
10 There are pandas in that cage, but they're having their afternoon sleep.
11 He was quite quiet.
12 We might have a picnic, but that depends on whether or not the weather stays good.
13 They had to dig deep holes in the ground the whole day long.
14 You simply need more practice – you must practise more.
15 Will you leave me in peace if I give you a piece of the cake?
16 She passed him in the street but she looked straight past him.
17 He was too tired to play two matches at the weekend.
18 Who's the student whose book was stolen?
19 I write with my right hand.
20 I know that I have made no mistakes now.

2.4 Phrasal verbs

Phrasal verbs consist of a verb and a particle (like *after, away, in, off, by, to*). In such a combination, a verb can change its meaning. For example, look at the following phrasal verbs with *to go*:

to go **away**	= to leave, to disappear
to go **by**	= to pass
to go **down**	= to sink, to fall
to go **in**	= to enter
to go **off**	= to explode; to stop working
to go **on**	= to continue
to go **up**	= to rise

2.5 Word formation: prefixes and suffixes

Like in German, you can expand basic words in English by adding syllables to the beginning of them ('prefixes') or to the end of them ('suffixes').

prefix	root or stem	suffix
under-	state	-ment

- The largest group of prefixes are those that make a word mean the opposite:

  anti- • dis- • in- / im- / ir- / il- • mis- • non- • un-

  e.g.: **anti**social • **dis**respectful • **im**possible • **in**capable • **ir**responsible • **il**legal • **mis**understanding • **non**sense • **un**believable

- Because there is usually no way of telling which root goes with which prefix, you need to check in a dictionary or do a an online search to see if you're right.

- Suffixes such as **-ly** or **-ness** are added to the end of a word to form a new word, e.g. *friendly* or *kindness*.

- Many abstract nouns are formed by adding a suffix to a verb or an adjective. Sometimes you need to change the spelling or the pronunciation, e.g. *produce* [prəˈdjuːs] or *production* [prəˈdʌkʃn].
  Here are six of the most common of these noun suffixes.

-ance, - ence	-ing	-ment	-ness	-tion, -ation	ty, -ity
exist**ence**	warn**ing**	argu**ment**	bright**ness**	pollu**tion**	equal**ity**

- Usually, *-ness* and *-ty / -ity* are added to adjectives, and the other suffixes are added to verbs.

2.6 Numbers, letters, signs

Mathematical numbers

100	'a / one hundred'
1,010	'a / one thousand and ten'
10,100	'ten thousand, one hundred'
100,101	'a hundred thousand, one hundred and one'
1,000,000	'a / one million'
1,000,000,000	'a / one billion'

⚠ ▸ Remember that English numbers use a comma (,) where German uses a point (.) and vice versa:

We write	We say
6.501	'six point five oh one'
6,501	'six thousand, five hundred and one'

Serial numbers, account numbers, code numbers etc.
Say the numbers – including double numbers, e.g. *33* – one after the other. For a nought (0), say either 'oh' or 'zero'. (See below 'German "Null" in English'.)

We write	We say
18995001	'one – eight – nine – nine – five – oh – oh – one'

German "Null" in English

There are several ways of expressing German "Null" in English:

How many **noughts** (BE) / **zeros** (AE) are there in a million?	mathematical numbers
The name of this file is FMT1_**zero zero** (BE, AE).	IT applications
We won three – **nil** (BE) / **zero** (AE).	score in team games
The score's 15 – **love** (BE, AE).	score in tennis
It was ten degrees below **zero** (BE, AE) last night.	temperatures
... three – two – one – **zero** (BE, AE). Lift-off!	countdowns to start
My phone number's three – four – **oh** (BE) / **zero** (AE) – six.	series of numbers, e. g. phone numbers

⚠ ▸ **Zero** is becoming much more common in BE, particularly in technical contexts.

Basic mathematical terms

+	plus		$\neq$	does not equal / is different from
−	minus		$\approx$	is approximately equal to
x	multiplied by		>	is greater than
÷	divided by		<	is less than
=	is / equals		$^1/_3$	one third
$\sqrt{}$	square root		$^1/_4$	one quarter (BE) / one fourth (AE)
$^3\sqrt{}$	cube root		$^9/_{10}$	nine tenths
4^2	four squared		$^{19}/_{64}$	nineteen over sixty-four
5^3	five cubed		**1.32**	one point three two
2^4	two to the power of four / two to the fourth		%	per cent (BE) / percent (AE)

Examples

We write	We say
2 + 3 = 5	two plus three is / equals five
9 − 6 = 3	nine minus six is / equals three
3 x 3 = 9	three multiplied by three is / equals nine
8 ÷ 2 = 4	eight divided by two is / equals four
5^3 = 125	five cubed is / equals one hundred **and** twenty-five
4^2 x 2^4 = 256	four squared multiplied by two to the power of four is / equals two hundred **and** fifty-six

Signs

xxx▾yyy	space		%	per cent (BE) / percent (AE)
xxx-yyy	hyphen ['haɪfn]		&	and / ampersand
xxx_yyy	underscore		*	asterisk
xxx / yyy	slash		#	hash
xxx // yyy	double slash		"	ditto
xxx \ yyy	backslash		=	equals
xxx.yyy	dot (internet, email)		!	exclamation mark
@	at		?	question mark
:	colon		,	comma
xxxy.	point (abbreviations)		;	semicolon
Gruber	big / capital letter		£	pound sterling
gruber	small letter		$	dollar
paulgruber	as one word		€	euro

Examples

jack.simmons@expressnet.com   jack **dot** simmons at expressnet **as one word, dot** com, all small

http://www.oeamtc.at   http **colon double slash** www **dot** oeamtc **dot** a-t, all small

kp560_8@hotpost.com   kp560 **underscore** 8 at hotpost dot com

2.7 Dates and times

■ In English, the 12-hour clock is used more often than the 24-four hour clock.

Examples

10:00	ten o'clock (in the morning) / ten (a.m.)
12:00	twelve (noon)
13:30	half past one (in the afternoon) / one thirty (p.m.)
13:45	a quarter to two (in the afternoon) / one forty-five (p.m.)
18:00	six o'clock (in the evening) / six (p.m.)
23:05	five minutes past eleven (at night) / eleven oh five (p.m.)
23:10	ten minutes past eleven (at night) / eleven ten (p.m.)
24:00	twelve o'clock at night / twelve (midnight)

■ When it is clear from the context whether you mean in the morning, afternoon or evening you can just say 'six o'clock', etc.

2.8 Dealing with technical English

- Technical English follows different rules from everyday or literary English: while the sentence structure may be quite simple, the heavy use of technical terms (usually nouns) can cause comprehension problems.

Word families

Knowing how English creates words can help you to recognize the meaning of unfamiliar expressions. Study the table:

Field	Person	Adjective
physics	physicist	physical
biology	biologist	biological
psychology	psychologist	psychological
genetics	genetecist	genetic
climatology	climatologist	climatological / climatic
biochemistry	biochemist	biochemical
meteorology	meteorologist	meteorological
astronomy	astronomist	astronomical
geology	geologist	geological
science	scientist	scientific

 ► physician = Arzt / Ärztin
► physicist = Physiker / in

Creating new words

- German usually forms compounds to describe a field more exactly, whereas English more often puts an adjective in front of the noun.

Look at the examples below.

German: compound	English: adjective + noun
Verhaltenspsychologie	behavioural psychology
Mondlandung	lunar landing
Strukturanalyse	structural analysis
Umwelttechnologie	environmental technology
Genmanipulation	... modification
Kernspaltung	... fission
Industriezeitalter	industrial age
Erdanziehungskraft	... force

 ► technique = method, way of doing sth
► technology = Technik

Like German, English forms complex terms by simply linking words together like railway carriages. However, these words are generally written separately, without a hyphen.

Engineering disciplines

English	German
mechanical engineering	*Maschinenbau*
electrical engineering	*Elektrotechnik*
constructional engineering	*Bauingenieurwesen, Hochbau*
aerospace engineering	*Luft- und Raumfahrttechnik*
agricultural engineering	*Agrartechnik*
automotive engineering	*Fahrzeugtechnik*
bioengineering	*Bioingenieurwesen*
chemical engineering	*Chemieingenieurwesen*
civil engineering	*Tiefbauwesen*
computer engineering	*technische Informatik*
environmental engineering	*Umwelttechnik*
industrial engineering	*Wirtschaftsingenieurwesen*
manufacturing engineering	*Fertigungstechnik*
materials engineering	*Werkstofftechnik*
mining engineering	*Bergbauingenieurwesen*

2.9 Irregular Verbs

Infinitive	Past	Past Participle	
to bear	bore	borne	*tragen; ertragen*
to beat	beat	beaten	*schlagen*
to become	became	become	*werden*
to begin	began	begun	*anfangen, beginnen*
to bend	bent	bent	*biegen*
to bet	bet / betted	bet / betted	*wetten*
to bite	bit	bitten	*beißen*
to bleed	bled	bled	*bluten*
to blow	blew	blown	*blasen*
to break	broke	broken	*brechen*
to bring	brought	brought	*bringen*
to broadcast	broadcast	broadcast	*senden, übertragen (im Rundfunk, Fernsehen)*
to build	built	built	*bauen*
to burn	burnt / burned	burnt / burned	*(ver)brennen*
to buy	bought	bought	*kaufen*
to cast (a vote)	cast	cast	*verteilen, werfen (Stimme abgeben)*
to catch	caught	caught	*fangen*
to choose	chose	chosen	*wählen*
to cling	clung	clung	*kleben, haften*
to come	came	come	*kommen*
to cost	cost	cost	*kosten*
to cut	cut	cut	*schneiden*
to deal	dealt	dealt	*sich beschäftigen*
to dig	dug	dug	*graben*
to do	did	done	*tun, machen*

Infinitive	Past	Past Participle	
to draw	drew	drawn	*ziehen; zeichnen*
to dream	dreamt / dreamed	dreamt / dreamed	*träumen*
to drink	drank	drunk	*trinken*
to drive	drove	driven	*fahren*
to eat	ate	eaten	*essen*
to fall	fell	fallen	*fallen*
to feed	fed	fed	*füttern*
to feel	felt	felt	*fühlen*
to fight	fought	fought	*kämpfen*
to find	found	found	*finden*
to flee	fled	fled	*flüchten*
to fly	flew	flown	*fliegen*
to forbid	forbade	forbidden	*verbieten, untersagen*
to forget	forgot	forgotten	*vergessen*
to freeze	froze	frozen	*(ge)frieren*
to get	got	got	*bekommen*
to give	gave	given	*geben*
to go	went	gone	*gehen*
to grow	grew	grown	*wachsen; anbauen; werden*
to hang	hung	hung	*hängen, aufhängen*
to hear	heard	heard	*hören*
to hide	hid	hidden	*(sich) verstecken*
to hit	hit	hit	*treffen, schlagen*
to hold	held	held	*halten*
to hurt	hurt	hurt	*verletzen*
to keep	kept	kept	*halten, behalten*
to know	knew	known	*wissen, kennen*
to lay	laid	laid	*legen*
to lead	led	led	*führen*
to learn	learnt / learned	learnt / learned	*lernen*
to leave	left	left	*verlassen*
to lend	lent	lent	*leihen, borgen*
to let	let	let	*lassen, zulassen*
to lie	lay	lain	*liegen*
to light	lit	lit	*anzünden*
to lose	lost	lost	*verlieren*
to make	made	made	*machen*
to mean	meant	meant	*bedeuten, meinen*
to meet	met	met	*treffen, begegnen*
to pay	paid	paid	*bezahlen*
to put	put	put	*setzen, stellen*
to quit	quit	quit	*verlassen*
to read	read	read	*lesen*
to ride	rode	ridden	*reiten, fahren*
to ring	rang	rung	*klingeln, anrufen*

Infinitive	Past	Past Participle	
to rise	rose	risen	*ansteigen; aufgehen*
to run	ran	run	*laufen*
to say	said	said	*sagen*
to see	saw	seen	*sehen*
to seek	sought	sought	*suchen, streben (nach)*
to sell	sold	sold	*verkaufen*
to send	sent	sent	*schicken, senden*
to set	set	set	*setzen, stellen*
to shake	shook	shaken	*schütteln*
to shine	shone	shone	*scheinen*
to shoot	shot	shot	*schießen*
to show	showed	shown	*zeigen*
to shut	shut	shut	*schließen*
to sing	sang	sung	*singen*
to sink	sank	sunk	*sinken, untergehen*
to sit	sat	sat	*sitzen*
to sleep	slept	slept	*schlafen*
to slide	slid	slid	*gleiten, rutschen*
to speak	spoke	spoken	*sprechen*
to spend	spent	spent	*ausgeben, verbringen*
to spill	spilt / spilled	spilt / spilled	*verschütten*
to spin	spun	spun	*spinnen*
to split	split	split	*spalten, teilen*
to spread	spread	spread	*verbreiten*
to stand	stood	stood	*stehen*
to steal	stole	stolen	*stehlen*
to stick	stuck	stuck	*kleben, stecken bleiben*
to stink	stank	stunk	*stinken*
to strike	struck	struck	*auffallen; schlagen*
to swear	swore	sworn	*fluchen; schwören*
to sweep	swept	swept	*fegen*
to swim	swam	swum	*schwimmen*
to swing	swung	swung	*schwingen*
to take	took	taken	*nehmen*
to teach	taught	taught	*unterrichten, lehren*
to tear	tore	torn	*(zer)reißen*
to tell	told	told	*erzählen*
to think	thought	thought	*denken, glauben*
to throw	threw	thrown	*werfen*
to understand	understood	understood	*verstehen*
to wake	woke	woken	*aufwecken, aufwachen*
to wear	wore	worn	*tragen*
to win	won	won	*gewinnen*
to write	wrote	written	*schreiben*

3 Communication skills

3.1 Expressing opinions

In discussion	In writing
I think / feel / believe (that) …	In my opinion …
It seems to me (that) …	In my view …
If you ask me …	My view of the matter is …

> ⚠ ► Ich meine, dass … = **I think that** …
> Not: ~~I mean that~~

3.2 Agreeing and disagreeing

Remember: agreeing and disagreeing with people can be very different in formal and informal situations.

Agreeing	Disagreeing
I agree (absolutely / 100 % / …).	I'm afraid I don't agree with you.
I think so too.	That's complete / absolute / … nonsense / …
Me too. / Me neither.	I understand what you're saying, but …
I couldn't agree more.	You've got to be joking!
That's right / true.	That's a good point, but have you thought about …?
Good point!	I don't think that's right.
That's exactly what I think.	That may be true, but I think …
You can say that again!	Hang on! / Wait a minute, …
Absolutely. / Of course.	I agree up to a point but then on the other hand …

3.3 Making comparisons

Look at the pictures and read the text below for a sample text of how to make comparisons in speaking.

1
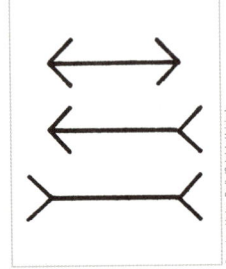

2
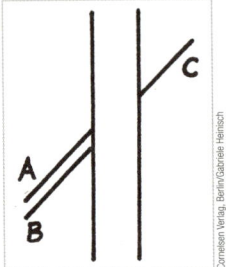

3

Now, take a look at the first drawing. As you can see, there are three horizontal lines, **the shortest on the top**, followed by **a slightly longer** one in the middle, and underneath that, **the longest of the three**. But is that really true? Well, no. The three lines are actually **the same length**.

But admittedly, the bottom line does **appear to be far longer than the other two**! Well, that's why it's called an optical illusion!

Now turn your attention to the second drawing. It's the one with the two parallel, vertical lines. You'll note that there are two slanted lines on the left, **one a bit higher than the other**. Now, the line on the right is the continuation of one of those lines – but which one?

If you're like most people, you'll say **the upper one. The lower one** appears to be **much too low** to connect with the line on the right. … Well, if you thought that, you'd be wrong.

If you take your ruler, you'll see that the upper line is **too high to connect** with the line on the right, but the lower line connects perfectly with it.

OK, now for the third drawing. How many colours do you see in it? Does anyone see **more or less than** four?

In fact, there are only two colours: one shade of green and one shade of pink. The two colours **only appear to be darker when they're next to each other**, not separated by white.

1 Study and language skills

1.1 Mind mapping

Mind mapping is useful for brainstorming and for trying to get either a general or a detailed view of a topic. You can also use it to plan a text or talk.

- ■ **Step 1:** Write the topic word or phrase in the middle of an empty, unlined piece of paper.
- ■ **Step 2:** Using different colours, draw branches and sub-branches out from the central word or phrase. Write words and phrases along these branches (not whole sentences) or use symbols, pictures or icons. You can add ideas at any stage.

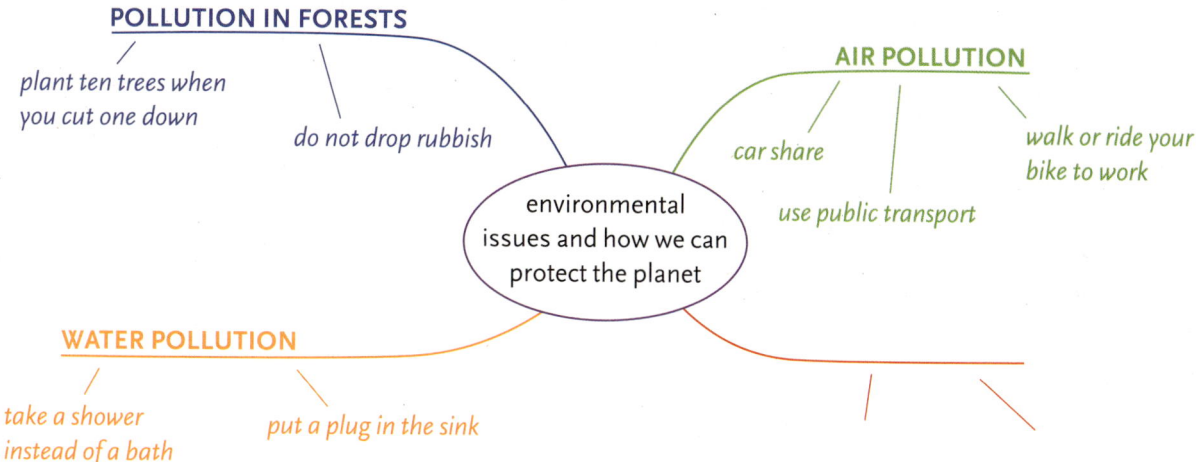

1.2 Brainstorming

Brainstorming is the first step in collecting your ideas. It is useful when you want to write a text or plan a talk. You can brainstorm on your own or in a group.

Individual Brainstorming

- ■ **Step 1:**
  Write down every idea that comes into your head on the topic you want to write or talk about.

  > Environment
  > - pollution
  > - protect nature
  > - WWF / Greens
  > - damage –> crisis
  > - recycling
  > - eco-friendly

- ■ **Step 2:**
  Choose those ideas you really want to explore further and structure them in a way you find helpful, e.g. in a mind map or in a chart with the 5 W's (the question who?, what?, when?, where? and why?).

who?	what?	when?	where?	why?
WWF – World Wide Fund for Nature	one of the biggest international non-governmental organizations	founded in 1961	in Switzerland	preserve biological diversity

Group brainstorming – the placement method

One of many different ways to brainstorm in a group is using the placemat method. You can see an example of a placemat on the right.

- **Step 1:**
  Get into groups of four. Everyone writes down at least three ideas on the topic in one of the four corners of the placemat.

- **Step 2:**
  Together, discuss all the ideas and choose the ones you agree are best or most important.

- Write them in the middle of your placemat.

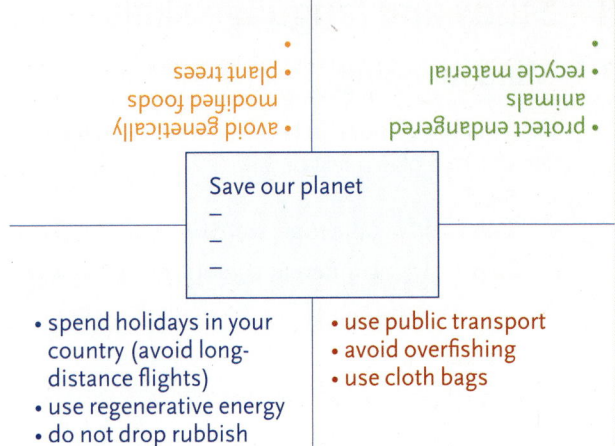

Placemat activity

1.3 Marking up a text

Marking up a text is useful if there is information in a text you're reading that you may want to look up later. Remember: You can only mark up texts in photocopies or in books that belong to you.

- **Step 1:**
  As you read the text, keep in mind what it is you need to know. When you find that information in the text, mark it by underlining, circling or highlighting it. Mark only keywords.

- **Step 2:**
  When you look over the passages you have marked, you may find it helpful to add keywords in the margins.

- **Step 3:**
  This way, when you need to find the information again, for example while preparing for a test, you only have to read the marked words and your notes in the margins.

What you can do to save the Earth:

1. **Recycle** newspapers, plastic and paper bags, aluminum cans, office and notebook paper, car oil, anything and everything at recycling centres, supermarkets, and petrol stations. It's a bit of an effort but it makes a huge difference.

   recycling

2. **Plant a tree.** Trees take carbon dioxide out of the air and give us oxygen to breathe.

3. **Take cloth bags** to the supermarket, especially when you are only buying a few things. Avoid using another plastic or paper bag. Use cloth rags and sponges instead of paper towels.

   use bags more than once

4. **Walk** if it's close, or take a bus or train or the underground. Cars pollute a lot.

   public transport

1.4 Taking notes

Taking notes ('*protokollieren*', '*mitschreiben*') is useful when you want to remember things you read or heard about, i.e. you write down someone else's ideas. It is, for example, helpful to take notes if you need to remember the key points of a classmate's talk or to get information from a recorded message.

- **Step 1:**

  Look or listen for keywords. These are words or phrases that contain the information you need to answer a question or that seem important in a passage.

- **Step 2:**

  Note down the keywords or ideas. Remember:
  - Don't write whole sentences:

    NOT: *The world population will increase to 9.2 billion by 2100.*

    BUT: *World pop. R 9.2 bill. (2100)*
  - Use numbers, abbreviations and symbols. You can make up your own abbreviations and symbols – but don't overdo it.

common abbreviations and symbols			
the same as	=	between	*bet.*
not the same as	≠	for example	*e.g.*
about the same as	≈	important	*impt.* or *!*
and	+	not	*x* or *ô*
and so on, et cetera	*...* or *etc.*	with	*w.* or *w /*
becomes / will be	→	without	*w /o*

1.5 Making notes

Making notes ('*Notizen machen*', '*sich Stichwörter notieren*') is useful for organizing information, i. e. when you put your own ideas on paper in short form. You make notes, for example, when you're preparing to write a text or structuring your ideas for a presentation.

When you make notes:

- use keywords, symbols and abbreviations, as in taking notes above.
- leave room to add more notes later. It is a good idea to leave a wide margin.
- treat your notes as a process. You can add ideas at any time, preferably in a different colour: use arrows (→) to make connections between ideas, and numbers to put your notes in a different order.

1.6 Dealing with words you don't know

Dealing with words you don't know (or have forgotten) is something you have to do all the time when you're learning and using a foreign language. There are lots of ways to find out what a word means, so don't panic.

- When you're reading / listening to a long text, you don't need to understand every word.
- Watch out for similarities between the unknown word and a word you already know in English, German or another language. But be careful: the words might be 'false friends'. (see p. 22, *False friends*)
- Check whether you know parts of the word. Sometimes a prefix or suffix may have been added to a word you already know.
- Use the context, as well as the title or heading, subtitles and pictures. This helps you work out what the meaning of a word might be.

1.7 Paraphrasing

Paraphrasing is useful when you don't know an English word that you need to use in conversation. It allows you to get across the meaning of the word without using the word itself.

Here are some tips:
- You can use synonyms: *(to begin) It's the same as 'to start'.*
  and antonyms: *(to win) It's the opposite of 'to lose'.*
- You can use a general word or phrase and then explain what the thing does, what it can be used for or where you can find it. You can also use a relative clause.
  (A drill) is a machine for making holes in the ground. People use it to get oil.
  (A desert) is an area where it's very dry and not much grows.
  (A volunteer) is a person who offers to work and help people, but doesn't ask for any money in return.

unknown word	paraphrase	strategy
smack	= hit	synonym
doubt	<–> believe	antonym
trout, pikeperch, salmon	different kinds of fish	general word
current	movement of water in the sea	what the thing is / does
lawnmower	a device for cutting grass in the garden	what it can be used for
exodus	a situation in which many people leave a place at the same time	relative clause

1.8 Working with pictures

Different kinds of pictures (photos, cartoons, posters, graphs and charts) can help you to understand something you are reading or listening to. They are also useful for getting a message across, e.g. in a presentation.

cartoon

poster

Describing a picture

When you are asked to describe a picture, don't give your opinion.

- **Step 1:** Read the title or caption first. Then look carefully to see what the main theme of the picture material is.

The	picture photo cartoon poster chart	is about … shows … provides proof of … illustrates …

Tip

When we describe a picutre, we describe what is happening at a moment in time – present progressive.

- **Step 2:** Always describe picture material systematically, e.g. from foreground to background, from top to bottom, from left to right.

In the centre In the foreground In the background At the very top In the left bottom corner	of the picture of the photo	you can see … we see … there is / there are … we can find …
	Underneath that On the left	

Analysing a picture

When you are asked to analyse a picture, you will be expected to draw conclusions about what the picture is trying to do, whether it does so effectively, and how it achieves its effect. The best way to analyse a picture is to ask yourself some questions and note down your answers.

- **For a picture / photo**

  What is the artist / photographer trying to say? How do they say it (technique / colours / …)? What effect does it have on the viewer / me?

  - The picture / photo clearly shows that …
  - It's a good a example of …
  - … is very attractive because …
  - … makes the point that …

A sample description:

The photograph shows two young men fighting or threatening each other. The young man on the left is holding a knife. The other young man on the right doesn't seem to be holding any weapon. In the background you can see some other people watching. Their facial expressions are strange. They aren't showing any emotion at all. Normally you would expect people to be shocked or scared. It looks to me as if they are acting in a play.

■ **For a poster / cartoon**

Who was it made for (newspaper, charity, political or advertising campaign)? Where and when did it appear? What is it trying to say / criticize / encourage people / me to do?

> ■ The poster / cartoon was meant to show voters / readers of the paper ...
> ■ It's very eye-catching through its use of ...
> ■ It speaks to the reader directly by ...ing ...
> ■ The layout / use of colour ...
> ■ ... is criticizing / making fun of ...

1.9 Working with charts and graphs

When researching a topic, you will frequently come across statistics which are presented using a chart or graph. Moreover, when giving a presentation, you may find it useful to present figures you have found in a chart or graph.

a pie chart

The relative numbers of native English speakers in major English speaking countries

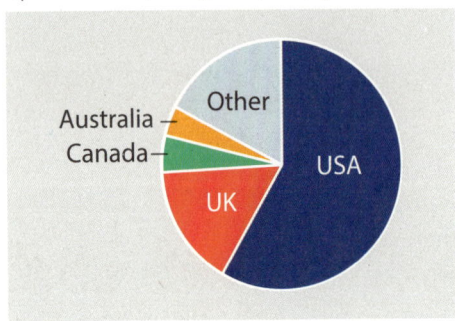

Data from: http://en.wikipedia.org

a bar chart

Austrians' favourite holiday destinations 2011

Data from: Statistik Austria

a line graph:

weather conditions in Sydney, Australia

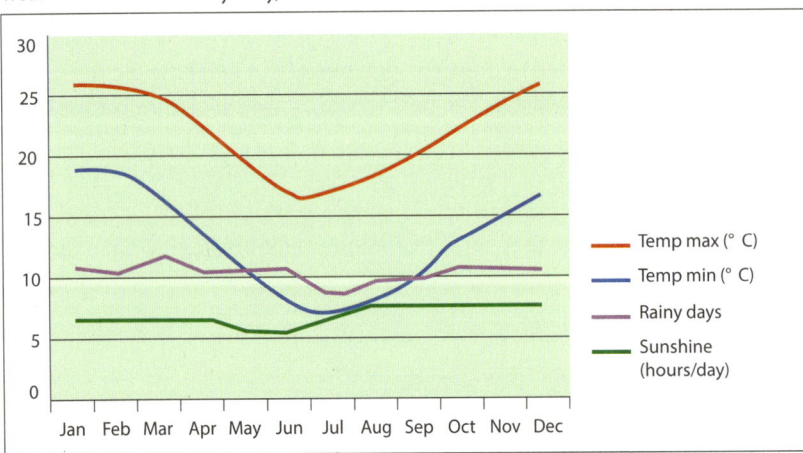

Source: http://www.aussieworld.com

When describing charts or graphs:

- **Step 1:** Open by saying what the the chart or graph is about (watch out for headlines, keys and axis labels [= *Legende*]).

- **Step 2:** Describe the statistical trends shown. Best begin with the extremes (the highest / the lowest figures). Mention any trends you find particularly interesting or surprising.

- **Step 3:** Close by summarizing the most important information. Wherever possible, draw a conclusion or refer to possible further developments.
  Always state the source of your figures.

Useful language for talking about graphs, charts and statistics

- The line graph deals with / shows the relationship between labour costs and productivity from 2010 to 2015 / …

- The bar chart compares the pay of men and women in manufacturing from 1995–2015.

- The pie chart deals with / shows the distribution of seats in the House of Representatives after the last election / …

- The line rises gradually / slowly / steeply / fast and peaks at / reaches a peak at …

- The line falls … and bottoms out at …

- The graph shows / illustrates a steady / sharp increase / rise / decrease / fall in profits over the last two / … years / …

- The pie chart is divided into four / … segments showing the sale of mobile phones / … to 15- to 25-year-olds / … during 2018 / …

- The pie chart shows the distribution of jobs in manufacturing and service industries in Austria / …

- The statistics present data on youth unemployment in the EU at the end of 2018.

- According to official / UN / … statistics, poverty is increasing in Africa / …

- The statistics on / relating to outsourcing to Asia suggest that …

- The statistics / figures are misleading because they do not include / take account of …

Useful verbs to describe (a / an) …

upward trend	downward trend	variation	no change
to climb to	to decrease	to fluctuate	to remain stable
to go up to	to drop	to vary	to level off
to increase	to go down to		
to jump to	to plunge to		
to peak	to fall to		
to reach a peak at	to bottom out at		
to reach an all-time high			
to rise			

■ **A sample chart description:**

(Note that this graph combines elements of a bar chart as well as those of a line graph.)

This graph by statistics.gov.uk shows how many people have immigrated to and emigrated from the United Kingdom between 1997 and 2006.

The orange line represents the development of immigration figures to the UK. It shows a steady increase from 300,000 in 1997 to almost 500,000 by the year 2000. Between 2000 and 2001 the number of immigrants remained fairly constant with another increase to slightly over 500,000 in 2002. From 2004 the line shows a sharp upturn, peaking just under 600,000. After that, there is the first slight decline, with another upward movement in 2006.

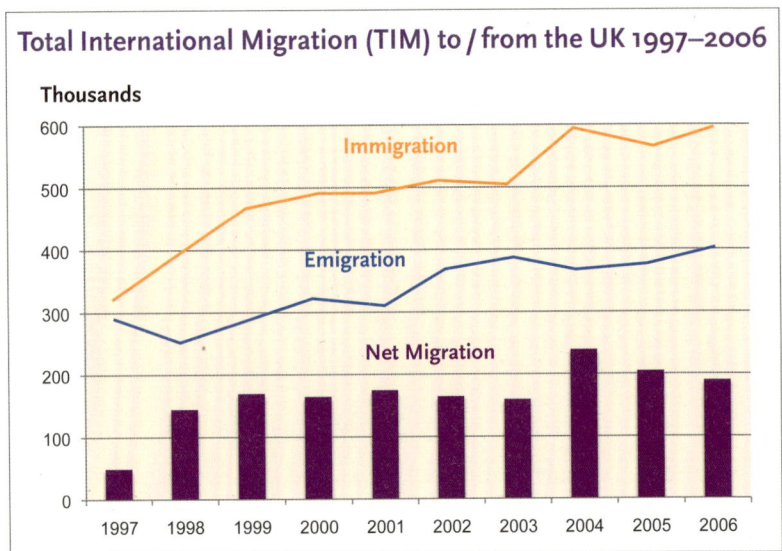

Total International Migration (TIM) to / from the UK 1997–2006

Data from: http://www.statistics.gov.uk

The blue line illustrates the development of emigration figures in the same period of time. At first there is a slight decrease in emigration numbers for the year 1998, but then we see a fairly steady increase; between 2002 and 2004 emigration figures were fairly stable around 360,000, even falling very slightly in 2004, but increasing up to 400,000 by 2006.

The bars represent the number of net migration, i.e. the number of immigrants left after the number of emigrants has been subtracted.

This shows that while the number of emigrants was always significantly lower than that of immigrants, both lines seem parallel for much of the time covered by the graph.

2   Listening skills

2.1 Listening for gist

Listening for gist is the skill you need when you're trying to a get a general picture of a spoken text quickly. Maybe you want to find out if something really is of use or interest to you.

■ **Step 1:** Before listening, make notes on
  – what you need to find out.
  – what you expect to hear in the text.
  – what words might help you.
  If you want to know the end of a story, you could make notes on the names of key characters and events.

■ **Step 2:** While you are listening, just concentrate on the areas you want to know about. You don't need to understand every word. The atmosphere, sound effects and tone of voice may help you. Take brief notes.

■ **Step 3:** As soon as you've finished listening, complete your notes.

2.2 Listening for detail

When you have to listen for detail, you need to be able to pick out specific information and understand it completely.

- **Step 1:** Before listening, make notes on the exact questions you need to answer and note down vocabulary that might help you. For example, if you need to find out from a radio interview in which year someone won an award, note down the person's name and the name of the award.

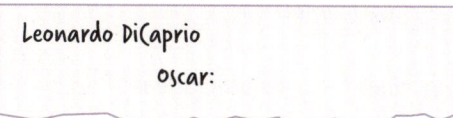

Leonardo DiCaprio

      Oscar:

- **Step 2:** While listening, focus on the names or keywords you have written down. Take notes on the specific information you need. If you're listening to a long text, interview or speech, watch out for signal words that might alert you to the information you need.

list of items, reasons:	*and, another, too*
counter arguments:	*although, but*
reasons for something, consequences of something:	*because, so, so that*
comparisons:	*bigger / older / more often / … than*
chronology:	*before, after, later*

- **Step 3:** Check that you've got and understood the details you need. Listen again if you need to. Check your notes and complete them.

3 Speaking skills

3.1 Giving a presentation

Giving a presentation is a skill that you need both at school and in later life (work, college, university, etc.).

Step 1: Preparing your presentation
- Research your subject, and make notes in English.
- Check your English and look up words that you find difficult to pronounce in a dictionary.
- Think of ways to make the talk more interesting, e.g. by using visuals, jokes, etc. Visualizing facts and figures can be a big help to your audience. When you are presenting statistics, a bar chart or pie chart may make them more attractive and easier to understand.
- If you want to offer your audience a handout, prepare it now too. The handout should include the main points of your presentation and can offer additional material (statistics, sources, pictures, etc.). You should structure the handout clearly. Headings and tables can help here. Leave room for your audience to write notes on it.
- You can also use electronic media, e.g. a presentation software such as PowerPoint.
  – Make sure the font you use is large enough so that the audience can read it.
  – Only write one aspect on each slide.
- Check that all the equipment you need is available.
- Practise your presentation in front of a friend or mirror.

Step 2: Giving your presentation

- Start by greeting the audience and by explaining the topic and structure of your presentation.
  Hello everybody and welcome to my presentation.
  I'm going to talk about ...
  I've divided my material into three parts. The first is about ..., the second is about ..., and the third is about ...
- Keep your presentation simple. Speak slowly and clearly.
- Stand up straight and face the audience, always keeping eye contact with them.
- At the end summarize the important points.
  So, / Just to remind you, here are the main points again: Firstly / Number one ...
- Ask your audience if they have any questions.
  That's the end of my presentation. Thank you for listening. Have you got any questions?

Useful phrases for presentations:

Beginning a presentation ➤	Giving an overview ➤	Signposting a presentation
■ First, I'd like to welcome you to my presentation. ■ My name's ... and I'm going to speak about ... ■ So let's start with ... ■ First, I'm going to ... ■ What I'd like to do this morning / afternoon / evening is ...	■ The presentation consists of five parts. ■ The subject of my presentation is ... ■ Now I'm moving on to ...	■ This brings me to ... ■ Let me now move on to ... ■ As I explained earlier, ... ■ Finally, I hope to show you that ...
Referring to visuals ➤	Asking for action ➤	Ending a presentation
■ Now let's look at the figures for ... ■ As you can see from ... , I'm going to ... ■ As this poster shows you ... ■ On page ... of your handout you can see ... ■ I'd now like to give a short visual presentation on ...	■ I'd be happy to answer any questions that you may have. ■ Can we have a show of hands, please? ■ If you have any questions, perhaps you would like to ask them now? ■ Have you got any questions? ■ Well, what about ... ?	■ So, summing up, we can say ... ■ That completes my overview. ■ That's the end of my presentation. ■ Thank you for giving me your time. ■ Thank you for coming in such large numbers. ■ Thank you for listening / for your attention.

3.2 Taking part in a classroom discussion

Having classroom discussions is a great way to exchange ideas and opinions with your classmates and to practise your English at the same time. A good discussion needs to be well-prepared and well-conducted.

- **Step 1:** Each person collects information on the chosen topic in order to back up their opinion. Research aspects that interest you in books, on the internet, in newspapers and magazines, etc. Make notes.

- **Step 2:** Organize your notes. Maybe you want to have material ready to show during the discussion.

- **Step 3:** Choose a discussion leader.

- **Step 4:** Start the discussion. Remember to listen carefully to what other people say. Whenever you can, refer to their points when you speak.

- **Step 5:** At the end of the discussion, the discussion leader summarizes the conclusions you have reached. Listen carefully and correct the summary if necessary.

Useful words and phrases

- **Making a point:** Before the discussion begins, make notes on your reaction to the topic. When the discussion starts, be ready to express your opinion. Make your own view clear.

  - I think ... / I feel ... / In my opinion ... / I (can't) believe ...
  - The fact is that ... / The point is that ...

- **Adding a point:** Follow up what has been said before.

  - I think ... is right because another thing that happens is that ...
  - What's more, ... / Furthermore, ...
  - We shouldn't forget that ...

- **Backing up a point:** Give reasons for your opinion, offering evidence – facts, quotations, figures, ...

  - I thought people were exaggerating, but look at ...
  - I really don't think you can argue with these facts. Look ...
  - I agree with ... / That's true. / That statement is right because ...
  - Here's an example of what I mean: ... / These figures prove my point: ...
  - The Chancellor has just said in an interview that ...
  - Firstly, ... Secondly, ...

- **Disagreeing:** Remember to be polite when you wish to express a different opinion.

  - I'm afraid I don't agree with ...
  - Sorry, those facts aren't correct.
  - I don't accept ... / I think it's wrong to say ..., because ...
  - ... talked about ..., but what about ...?

- **Expressing uncertainty:** Say you're unsure about what someone else has said.

  - I'm not clear about ..., but I think that ...
  - ..., you said ..., but surely all ... think ..., don't they?

- **Asking for clarification:** If you have misunderstood or not heard what has been said, ask the person to repeat it.

  - I'm sorry, ..., I didn't understand that – can you say it again, please?
  - Could you repeat that, please? I'm not sure I understood what you said.
  - Excuse me, but did you mean that ...?

- **Summarizing:** At the end of the discussion, summarize your views.

  - So, to sum up, ...
  - That's why I think ...
  - So there can't be any doubt that ...
  - In a nutshell ...

3.3 Making conversation

One of the most important skills you will need whenever you're talking to people in English is the skill of making conversation. If you just remember a few points, you'll come across as polite and friendly and you'll find that you can avoid a lot of the stress in meeting new people, whether in a formal or an informal situation.

Step 1:   A friendly start
  formal: *Hello! / Good morning. / How do you do? / I'm pleased to meet you.*
  informal: *Hi! I'm new here. My name's … / Hi there! Is it OK if I sit here?*

Step 2:   Keeping the conversation going
  ■ Avoid one-word answers.
    It's nice to meet you too. / My name's …
    Yes, of course you can. / No, I'm sorry but …
    Yes, thank you. / Fine, thank you.
  ■ Follow an answer or a statement with another question wherever you can.
    What about you? / And you? / What do you think? / Do you like …? / Have you … yet?
  ■ Respond to questions.
    Well, I'm interested in … too. / I often … too. / I like … a lot.

Step 3:   A friendly ending
  formal: *Well, I hope to see you at the … then. / It was nice talking to you.*
  informal: *Bye, then. / See you later.*

3.4 Everyday English: functional language

Telephoning for accommodation

Useful phrases
- I'm calling from …
- I'd like to make a reservation for …
- I'd like a single / double / … room for … nights.
- We'll be staying … nights, from …to …
- Do I need to confirm the reservation?
- Do I have to pay a deposit?
- Can I pay by cheque / credit card?
- Do you accept international youth hostel cards?
- Is there a bus that stops somewhere nearby?

Travelling by public transport

Useful phrases
- What time is the next bus / train / coach to …?
- When does the next bus / train / coach to … leave?
- How much is a single / return ticket to …?
- Do I need to reserve a seat?
- Can I take my bicycle with me?
- Does this bus / train / coach go to …?
- What is the next stop?
- Where do I need to get off?

Going shopping

Useful phrases
- Excuse me, I'm looking for a …
- Can I try this / these … on, please?
- Do you have this / these in a different size / colour?
- How much is / are the …?
- I'll take it / them.
- Can I pay cash / by credit card / debit card?
- too tight / loose / baggy
- too long / short
- wrong colour / style
- too expensive
- It's broken / got a tear / stain.
- Something seems to be missing.
- The zip / lock / battery doesn't work.

Eating out / Making informal appointments

Useful phrases
- Do you want to eat out tonight?
- I've heard there's a great ... restaurant in ... Why don't we go and try it?
- Do you like Vietnamese food?
- OK, why not?

- When shall we meet?
- How about 8 o'clock? Is that OK / too late / early?
- No, that's fine.
- Shall we meet at the restaurant?
- Is it OK if ...?
- OK, we'll see you there.

Making an emergency call

Useful phrases
- What's your emergency?
- Where are you? / What is your location?
- Are you hurt? / Are there any casualties?
- How many people have been hurt?
- Are they conscious / breathing?

- What has been lost / stolen?
- What does it look like? Can you describe ...?
- Are you calling from a mobile telephone?
- Can you give me your number, please?

3.5 Using the appropriate register

Compare the three statements in the speech bubbles. What have they got in common? In what way(s) do they differ?

Much as I would like to oblige, I regret that I am presently occupied.

I'd really love to help, but unfortunately I'm very busy today.

I'd give you a hand, mate, but I ain't got a minute to spare.

- Register refers to differences in language based on the situation and the people involved. Different registers are used in different situations; for example, an informal register is used for a chat on the phone, whereas a business letter requires a formal register.
- When you write an essay, aim for a neutral or moderately formal register.
- A good dictionary will have *style labels* like the following to mark words which are not neutral.

formal expressions are usually only used in serious or official language and would not be appropriate in normal everyday conversation. Examples are *admonish*, *besmirch*.

informal expressions are used between friends or in a relaxed or unofficial situation. They are not appropriate for formal situations. Examples are *bonkers*, *dodgy*.

literary language is used mainly in literature and imaginative writing, for example *aflame*, *halcyon*.

offensive expressions are used by some people to address or refer to people in a way that is very insulting, especially in connection with their race, religion, sex or disabilities, for example *half-caste*, *slut*. You should not use these words.

slang is very informal language, sometimes restricted to a particular group of people, for example people of the same age or those who have the same interests or do the same job. Examples are *dingbat*, *dosh*.

taboo expressions are likely to be thought by many people to be obscene or shocking. You should not use them. Examples are *bloody*, *shit*.

Source: Oxford Advanced Learner's Dictionary

4   Reading skills

4.1 Skimming (reading for gist)

This skill is useful for quickly finding out what a long text is about, i.e. reading for gist. Use it to decide whether or not to read a text more closely. Skimming will also help you to get an overview of a text's structure so that you'll understand it better when you read it.

- **Step 1:** First look at the title, any words in bold print, pictures and their captions.
- **Step 2:** Then look at the first and last sentences of each paragraph. The first sentence of the paragraph is usually the topic sentence and will give you the main idea of the paragraph.
- **Step 3:** Don't read every sentence in detail.

4.2 Scanning (reading for detail)

This skill is useful for finding specific information in a longer text without having to read the whole text, i.e. reading for detail.

- **Step 1:** Decide which keyword or short phrase might help you to find the parts of the text that contain the information you are looking for.
- **Step 2:** Make a mental picture of the keyword or phrase as it would look on the page.
- **Step 3:** Keeping your mental picture in mind, move your eyes quickly over the printed page. You can use your finger to guide your eyes. Don't try to read the text. You will find that the words you're looking for will 'jump out at you'.
- **Step 4:** After you have located relevant parts of the text, read them for the information you need. Scan the text again if you have to – either for the same keyword or phrase or for different ones.

5   Writing skills

5.1 The stages of writing

Writing involves many different skills. Following these steps will help you to produce better written texts.

The planning stage

- **Step 1:** Brainstorm your topic. It's better to have too many ideas than too few.
- **Step 2:** Define your topic. It's important that you know what it is you want or need to write about. Be clear in your mind who you are writing for and why. Do you want to convince your readers of something, inform them or simply entertain them?
- **Step 3:** Organize the ideas you've collected. Decide which ones you will include in your text. Decide on an order for presenting your ideas and then write an outline or make a mind map with numbers to show the order.

The first draft stage

- **Step 1:** Do your research. What do you need to know more about? Find out about it. As you learn more about your topic, you might have to adjust your plan.
- **Step 2:** Write a first, rough draft. Following your outline or mind map, write down what you want to say. Don't worry about correctness or the best way of saying something at this stage. You can even write a word in German if you can't think of the English expression. Leave lots of room on the page to make corrections later.
- **Step 3:** Write out your first draft. Read what you have written and make first improvements. Use your dictionary to find the English expressions for things you've written in German. Write out your text again clearly, leaving room for adding and correcting later.

- **Step 4:** Do something else if possible. Go for a walk or listen to music. The main thing is: take your mind off your writing. When you come back, you will see things you didn't see before.

The revision stage

- **Step 1:** Read your work. Read what you have written without making any changes to it. When you have finished, think about it: Is it logical? Does it say everything you want to say? Is everything in the right order? Go back and make any necessary changes.
- **Step 2:** Proofread your work. Read your text slowly and carefully. Check the content, style, grammar, spelling and punctuation. Use your learning log to help you look for your 'favourite' mistakes. You may have to read the text several times, looking for only one or two things each time. Asking a partner to check your work is a good idea.
- **Step 3:** Rewrite your piece. Make a clean copy of your work.

5.2 Writing an outline

This skill is useful for organizing information. It's a more formal way of making notes. You can use it to examine the structure of a text you have read or to plan a presentation or a text that you want to write.

The structure of an outline

- An outline is arranged so that you can quickly see what's most important. The most important ideas are farthest to the left.

```
Title
I. Main idea 1
    A. Important fact
            1. Supporting fact
            2. Supporting fact
                    a. Example or detail
                    b. Example or detail
    B. Important fact
II. Main idea 2
```

- All 'main ideas' are of equal importance, as are the 'important facts', etc.
- The 'main ideas' often correspond to whole sections of the text, the 'important facts' to individual paragraphs.
- Use keywords when writing an outline.

5.3 Writing a summary

Writing a summary is effective for passing on the content of a long text, film, play or listening piece. You need to include the most important information, but also to be brief.

- **Step 1:** Listen to / Read the text, or watch the film clip you want to summarize at least once. Then state in one or two sentences what the piece is about (the main idea). Use the present tense.
  The article is about the problems immigrants are facing just after their arrival in their new home country.
- **Step 2:** Use the five W's (the questions **who?**, **what?**, **when?**, **where?** and **why?**) to make notes or a mind map about the text. Write down only the things you think someone needs to know about your text in order to understand what it's about.
- **Step 3:** Use your notes to write a first draft of your summary. Don't use quotes or examples from the original. Use your own words, but don't give your opinion on anything.
- **Step 4:** Revise your draft. If you have been told to use a certain number of words for your summary, count the words. In case you need to reduce the number of words, make sure you have explained things and cut examples from the text.
- **Step 5:** Prepare your final draft. It should contain all the important points and read well.

5.4 Structuring a text

This skill is useful for writing any kind of text. Your readers will be able to follow your thoughts better if you structure them logically.

- Different kinds of texts require different structures. For example, to tell a story or to report on something, you might want to relate events in the order they occur, i.e. in 'chronological order'. To convince others of something, you might want to give your best arguments first, then the less important ones.

- There are a few general rules for ordering a text. Every longer text should have a clear beginning, middle and an end.

  – The **beginning** needs to state clearly what the text is about. It can consist of one or more introductory paragraphs and should awaken the readers' interest. Some examples from different kinds of texts:

    - There are many possible reasons for migration. Here we will examine …
    - Yesterday Tottenham Road was the scene of a terrible accident in which many people were injured. …
    - When Jane woke up last Saturday, she knew it was going to be an unusual day. …

  – The **main part (body)** develops the ideas or relates the events.

    - An example of the problem I'm talking about can be seen …
    - The most common reason for leaving one's home country is …
    - A witness reported having seen …
    - After several minutes of this, Jane decided it was time to …

  – The **end** brings the text to a conclusion, usually in a paragraph or two. It is here that readers find out what conclusions you draw from the facts presented in the text, or what happens to the main character in the end, or where they are reminded of what you are trying to convince them of.

    - In conclusion, I believe it is clear that …
    - To sum up our survey of national and international migration, …
    - Considering the damage done to the cars involved, the victims are lucky that …
    - At the end of this amazing day, Jane …

- When you write your text, follow your outline.

5.5 Linking ideas

This skill is useful for making your writing easier to follow and, at the same time, more interesting. It allows you to improve your style of writing.

Types of connectors and how they are used:

- to show how your text is organized:

  - In the article, the writer describes how …
  - **Firstly**, he states that … . **Secondly**, …
  - **Then** he goes on to say that …
  - **Another point** he makes is that … .
  - **Finally**, …

- to give reasons for something:

  - **Due to / Because of / As a result of** increased immigration, …
  - … numbers rose sharply. **Therefore**, the government felt that it had to …
  - … had been in trouble with the law, **so** …

- to add ideas:

    - The author thinks her characters ... . **In addition,** / **Moreover,** she has given them ...
    - **In addition to** / **Besides** / **As well as** finding ..., the main character becomes ...

- to contrast two or more thoughts:

    - **Although** one could argue that ..., I believe ...
    - **Whereas** / **While** most people would ..., the Prime Minister has said ...
    - Serious scientists all agree that ... . **However,** / **But** some politicians still claim ...
    - **On the one hand,** there is a feeling that ... . **On the other hand,** it's clear that ...

- to give examples:

    - This is true in a number of cases, **for example** / **for instance** / **e.g.** ...

- to explain results and consequences:

    - **As a consequence,** / **All in all,** / **Consequently,** it is fair to say that ...
    - **To sum up,** / **To conclude,** / **In conclusion,** I would like to say ...

5.6 Finding alternatives to overused words

Everyday words like *be*, *do* and *have* are useful (and often necessary), but their frequent use can sometimes hurt your style. So it makes sense to look for alternatives. In addition to a monolingual dictionary, a thesaurus or the synonym function of your word processing program can help you to find suitable alternatives.

Here are some overused words and suggestions for alternatives:

good
Marilyn is regarded as a ~~good~~ **capable** worker.
The author names two ~~good~~ **convincing** arguments to support her position.
The measures adopted by the commission will all be ~~good~~ **beneficial** for the environment.

happy
Tom was ~~happy~~ **overjoyed** when he won the first prize.
The passengers were ~~happy~~ **relieved** that no one had been hurt in the crash.
The CEO wasn't ~~happy~~ **satisfied** with sales in the first quarter.

bad
She was worried because her parents were both in ~~bad~~ **poor** health.
Everyone knows that it's ~~bad~~ **harmful** to smoke.
We still have ~~bad~~ **unpleasant** memories of our last holiday in Spain.

to write about
In the first part of the book, the author ~~writes about~~ **describes** the conditions in the South just before the Civil War.
In her latest biography, Laura Thompson ~~writes about~~ **portrays** Agatha Christie, one of the most popular British authors of the last century.
In his editorial, Monbiot ~~writes about~~ **examines** the reasons for our unwillingness to change our comfortable lifestyles.

to say
The police ~~said~~ **reported** that about fifty people had gathered in the square.
Her ex-husband ~~said~~ **claimed** that he had been out of town the night of the murder.
The guide ~~said~~ **suggested** that we should visit the exhibition before touring the grounds.

to talk about
The panel will ~~talk about~~ **discuss** the pros and cons of nuclear power.
In this interview, George Clooney ~~talks about~~ **reveals** the secret of his success.
Between the songs, Bob Dylan ~~talked about~~ **recalled** the early days of his career as a protest singer.

5.7 Writing a paragraph

A paragraph is a group of related sentences that discuss **one main idea**. It may stand by itself or may be one part of a longer piece of writing such as an essay or a book.

The structure of a paragraph

A paragraph is structured like a "mini-essay", which means it has a **topic sentence** (usually the first sentence that states the main idea of the paragraph) and **supporting sentences** (add to the thought or illustrate it). Some paragraphs also have a **concluding sentence**, which signals the end of the paragraph and leaves the reader with the most important ideas to remember.

Important elements of a paragraph

An important element of a good paragraph is **unity**, which means that it discusses only one main idea. Sometimes it is possible to discuss more than one aspect of the same idea in one paragraph if they are closely related to each other. Moreover, unity means that every supporting sentence directly explains the main idea.

Another element of a good paragraph is **cohesion**, that means the sentences need to connect to each other and make up a whole. The movement from one sentence to the next must be logical and smooth without sudden jumps. Do not just write one sentence after another:

→ **see linking words, p. 46**

There's a lot of unrest in the country. People are worried about the economy.
BETTER: *There's a lot of unrest in the country because people are worried about the economy.*

Key features

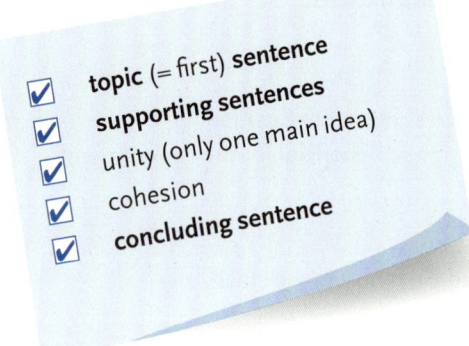

- [✓] topic (= first) **sentence**
- [✓] **supporting sentences**
- [✓] unity (only one main idea)
- [✓] cohesion
- [✓] **concluding sentence**

5.8 Writing an informal letter or email

When writing to friends and family or someone you know socially, there is a variety of (idiomatic and colloquial) expressions (including contractions, e.g. 'don't' instead of 'do not') we can use.

Informal letters or emails usually have five parts:

- the greeting (***Dear ..., Hi, Hello ...***)
- the introduction which is the first paragraph (***Thanks for your email / letter ..., How are You? I'm writing because ...***)
- the body which deals with the main subject, e.g. school / work, family, friends, holidays etc.
- the conclusion with its closing remarks (***That's all for now. Write soon! Give my regards to ...***)
- the signature line.

From: Nick and Sonya Carter
To: bradleyjowen1995@g-mail.com
[1]   **Subject:**   Re: See you Easter!

[2]   Hi Brad

[3]
+   Thanks for your email. It was great to hear from you and I'm really looking forward to your visit. **[6]**
[5]   It's been two years since my stay with your lovely family in Wisconsin. I can hardly believe it!

The first week of your stay, I'll still be in school. If you like, you can come to school with me and take part in classes. It would be great to have your help in my English class! Mom has checked with the school principal and it's OK for you to come to school with me – if you want to.

After that, it's the Easter holiday. Mom and Dad are going to Graz to visit Grandma and Grandpa. That wouldn't be much fun for you, so I've got another plan for us. We could go to the Salzkammergut and spend a week at our friends' holiday house. It's on the shore of a lake and we can go hiking and windsurfing. The water will be freezing but don't worry: I've got a thick wetsuit that will fit you.

If the weather's bad, we can go to Salzburg and hit the cafés and shops. It's also not far on the train to Linz. The Ars Electronica Center has a cool robotics exhibition at the moment and I'd really like to go, if you're interested in that sort of thing.

Remember that the weather can be quite changeable in Austria at Easter, so pack winter clothes as well as T-shirts.

[7]   That's all for now. See you soon!

[8]   All the best
[9]   Stefan

---

1   Subject line: a brief description of the reason for writing, e.g. *Looking forward to your visit!*
2   Salutation: *Hi Ben / Alice*
3   Start the body of the email with a capital letter.
4   Ask how the recipient is, e.g. *How are things? How are you? I hope you're well.*
5   If appropriate, thank the recipient for his / her email.
6   Use short forms, e.g. *I'm, you're, don't, can't.*
7   Finish your letter in a friendly way, e.g. *That's all for now / Please write soon / It would be great to hear from you.*
8   Close: *Bye for now / All the best / Take care*
9   Your name

5.9 A model CV

euro*pass*

Curriculum Vitae

PERSONAL INFORMATION	Gernot Mayer Beethovengasse 19 1090 Vienna, Austria +43 (0)660 400 1983 gt_mayer_03@gmx.com
Date of Birth	28 May 2003
Job applied for	Intern

WORK EXPERIENCE

4 August 2018 – 30 August 2018	Work placement North Cranes, Newcastle-upon-Tyne Assembly

EDUCATION AND TRAINING

2017 – present	Technical College Vienna will finish with *Reife- und Diplomprüfung* (school-leaving certificate – equivalent to A-levels)
2011 – 2014	NMS Glasergasse, Vienna (secondary school) School-leaving certificate (equivalent of GCSE)
2007 – 2011	Volksschule Marktgasse, Vienna Primary school

PERSONAL SKILLS

Mother tongue(s)	German

Other language(s)

	UNDERSTANDING		SPEAKING		WRITING
	Listening	Reading	Spoken interaction	Spoken production	
English	B1	B1	B1	B1	B1
Spanish	A2	A2–B1	A2	A2	A2

Social skills	Voluntary work experience with the Red Cross
Computer skills	Proficient with Microsoft Office programs (Word, Excel, PowerPoint, Outlook), Adobe Photoshop, Internet Explorer and competent with Linux
References	Can be supplied upon request

Based on: europass.cedefop.europa.eu

1 Listening and reading

1.1 Multiple choice

Reading comprehension: *multiple choice*

1 Read the questions – or statements with missing words – carefully before you start to answer.

2 Read all the alternative answers before deciding on one of them, even if you are sure that you have found the correct one (key) as the differences between the distractors (wrong answers) and the key are often subtle or tricky.

3 'Say' the sentences with the different solutions in your head. Often you'll find that one of them simply 'sounds' right, or that (some of) the others definitely sound wrong.

4 If you aren't sure of an answer, mark the question and go back to it later. Do not simply skip questions you are not sure about. Make educated guesses after a careful process of elimination.

---

 2 Listening comprehension: multiple-choice

11 **You are going to listen to Australian farmer Jack O'Donnell talking about the School of the Air. While listening, choose the correct ending (A, B, C or D) for sentences (1–6). Put a (X) in the correct box. The first one (0) has been done for you.**

0 Jack grew up …
   A in a small Outback town.
   B on a farm.
   C in Europe.
   D in the 1960s.

1 Jack's family home …
   A was hundreds of kilometres from the neighbours.
   B was very uncomfortable in winter.
   C was very hot in summer.
   D was hundreds of kilometres from a town.

2 Jack wasn't lonely because …
   A he could talk to his friends on the radio.
   B there were several other young people around.
   C he went to stay with his friends Megan and Annie.
   D his relations often came to visit.

0	A ☐	B X	C ☐	D ☐
1	A ☐	B ☐	C ☐	D ☐
2	A ☐	B ☐	C ☐	D ☐

Listening comprehension: *multiple choice*

This task checks that you can understand important information in a radio programme or recorded conversation between native speakers of English.

1 Read the task carefully before your first listening. That will give you an idea of the content of the recording and what information you should listen for.

2 During the first listening, get a general idea of what is being said. Do not worry about individual words that you do not know or did not hear properly.

3 Reread the task while listening and choose the best solutions.

4 As you listen a second time, check your answers.

1.2 True / false with justification

This is a **reading comprehension task** in which you have to answer questions by ticking true or false and then justify your choice with the first four words of the relevant sentence in the text.

---

2 Reading comprehension: true / false with justification

Read the text about Matty's room.

Decide whether the statements (1–8) are true (T) or false (F) and put a cross (**X**) in the correct box. Then identify the sentence in the text which supports your decision. Write the first four words of the sentence in the space provided. The first one (0) has been done for you.

0	Matty's room is untidy because he doesn't want to put things away.
1	Playing an instrument makes Matty happier when life is difficult.
2	Matty's sister enjoys his guitar music.
3	Matty plays in a rock band with some friends from school.

	T	F	First four words
0		X	My bedroom is too
1			
2			

⚠ ▸ Your answer will only be correct if you write exactly 4 words – not more (and not less)!

1.3 Multiple matching

Your task is to match questions, sentence halves or headings to different texts or sections of a text.

🎧 **1 Listening comprehension: multiple matching**

07   **Listen to the recording again. While listening, match the beginnings of the sentences (1–6) with the endings (A–I). There are two endings that you should not use. The first one (0) has been done for you.**

0	Some of Jade's schoolmates ___ .
1	Many think that trailer parks ___ .
2	In fact Jade finds that trailer park families ___ .
3	Thomas's family lived in a trailer park because his parents ___ .

E	were not trouble makers
F	had to leave the trailer park
G	didn't stay in the trailer park for long
H	don't respect Jade because she lives in a trailer
I	the trailers were too close to each other

	0	1	2	3	4	5	6
	H						

Listening comprehension: *multiple matching*

This task checks that you can understand the main ideas of a recorded conversation or talk in English.

1   Read the task carefully before your first listening. That will give you an idea of the content of the recording and what information you should listen for.
2   During the first listening, get a general idea of what is being said. Do not worry about individual words that you do not know or did not hear properly.
3   Reread the task while listening and choose the best solutions.
4   As you listen a second time, check your answers. Check that your solutions make grammatical sense as well as fitting the content.

Reading comprehension: *multiple matching*

The purpose of this task is to show that you can grasp the logical progression of a text and use grammatical and content clues.

1   Read the text and the sentence parts.
2   Try matching each part to each gap. Which ones make sense – also from a grammar point of view? Write their letters in the gap.
3   Make sure your choices make sense in the context.
4   Write your final answers in the boxes.

1.4 Note form

Your task is to answer questions, complete sentences or graphs in no more than four words. Four-word-answers don't require entire grammatically correct structures.

---

2 Reading comprehension: note form

Read the text 'A brand new home' on page 30 again. Answer the questions (1–6) using a maximum of four words. Write your answers in the space provided. The first one (0) has been done for you.

0	What have the Morettis just done?	moved into new house
1	Why do the Morettis need a big garden?	
2	How does Jan feel about the move from Darwin?	
3	How did the Morettis get the money for a big, new house?	

---

1 Reading comprehension: sentence completion

You are going to read a text about energy drinks and snacks. Complete the sentences (1–7) using a maximum of four words. The first one (0) has been done for you.

0	Energy drinks and snacks promise to give you extra _____	energy, nutrients
1	Energy drinks and nutrition bars may claim to help you to do better _____.	
2	TIt is probably safe to consume these products_____.	
3	They are popular because today's teenagers are_____.	

2 Speaking

2.1 Individual long turn

4 Speaking: individual long turn (4–5 minutes)
You want to work during your summer holidays.
The positions shown in the pictures might be available.

- Compare the two summer holiday jobs shown in the photos.
- Discuss points for and against each job.
- State what type of summer holiday job you would do and why.

The purpose of this task is to show that you can express your ideas clearly in English about a subject of general interest.

- You will have ten minutes to prepare. Use this time to note down some thoughts: write key words to help you remember what you want to talk about, not whole sentences.
- There are no 'right' or 'wrong' answers, so say what you think.
- Try not to repeat yourself.
- Stay on topic.
- The instructions will help you. Try to cover each point thoroughly before you move on to the next.
- You will get a lot more out of the topic if you consider both sides of everything:
  On the one hand … On the other hand …
- Use expressions to give yourself time to think: *Well, … It seems to me, … What I think is this …*
- Do not learn a text before the exam and then try to make it fit!
- Try to interest the examiner in what you are saying by making your voice lively and keeping eye contact.
- Speak clearly and remember to breathe!
- Do not try to be funny or tell jokes.

2.2 Interaction

> **5 Speaking: interaction (8 – 10 minutes)**
> **You are going to spend a weekend in London during the holidays, but you don't have much money to spend on accommodation.**
>
> - Discuss the following aspects:
>   - cost
>   - location
>   - security
>   - contact to local people
>   - comfort
> - Assess the advantages and disadvantages of your options: couchsurfing or a cheap hostel.
> - Come to an agreement with your partner about where to stay.

The purpose of this task is to show that you can conduct a conversation in English about an everyday topic. That includes expressing your own ideas and also asking another person's opinion and responding politely and appropriately to what he / she says.

- Speak clearly.
- Avoid repeating yourself.
- If you are running out of ideas, ask your partner a question.
- If you do not understand what your partner says, you can say 'Could you repeat that, please?' or 'Sorry, I don't quite understand.'
- To give yourself time to think, you can use 'fillers' like: 'Well, in my view …' and 'That's an interesting question …'
- Remember that this is supposed to be a conversation, not a monologue, so involve your partner: 'What do you think?'

2.3 What if I run out of words?

Here are some helpful phrases in case you get stuck during a presentation, (formal) conversation or a speaking test:

Sticking to the same point	Adding further details
■ Before going any further ….	… let's look at …
■ Before going over to the next question …	… I would like to add …
■ Before talking about this point …	… let me discuss …
■ What is more …	

If you can't think of an important word	If you don't know the answer
■ Perhaps this could also be described as …	■ Well, I don't know if this is exactly the answer you would like to have, but …
■ Sorry, I got stuck: what I need is the word for …	■ I'm not so sure about that, but what I do know is …
■ May I ask you for the meaning of …	
■ I'm thinking of something that …	
■ … could be compared to (a / an)…	
■ … looks / sounds like ..	
■ … is used for …	
■ … is similar to …	

If you want to win some time or want to make sure you've understood correctly	Clarifying a point
■ Am I right in thinking (that) …?	■ What I really mean is …
■ So do you mean (that) …?	■ My point is that …
■ Is the general / basic idea …?	■ What I'm trying to say is …
■ What I've heard now is (that) …?	■ Let me clarify / explain …

3 Writing: text formats

3.1 Letters / emails

Application (letter of motivation / covering letter)

Definition	In a letter of application you reply to an advertisement for a vacant position.
Purpose	You are applying for a job, so you need to advertise yourself and your skills. Form and content have to be convincing.
Target group	The recipient of the letter is mentioned in the advertisement. Consider the following points: Who is this person / company? What are his / her expectations? How can I create interest with my application?
Structure	■ **Salutation:** formal, i.e. *Dear Ms X / Dear Mr Y* or *Dear Sir or Madam* (if you don't have a name) [1] ■ **Introduction:** refer to the advertisement. [2] ■ **Main part:** give your qualifications, experience and your motivation to apply for the job. [3] ■ **Ending:** say when and how you can be contacted, express hope to hear from the other person. [4] ■ **Complimentary close,** signature, name. [5]
Style	formal language

Elisa Herbst
Schulgasse 30
1180 Vienna
Austria

Mrs. K. Beggs
HR Department
Priority Business Iowa
Prairie Drive
Des Moines, IA 97802
USA

August 28, 20..

Application for the position of human resources assistant #423

[1] Dear Mrs. Beggs,

[2] I am writing to express my interest in your current opening for a human resources assistant. Having researched the services, goals and culture of your company, I am excited by the possibility of working for you.

[3] As a recent graduate of an Austrian business college, I believe I am a strong candidate for this position.

Your advertisement specifies that you are looking for someone with excellent communication and organization skills. As an English language tutor, an administrative intern for an international nongovernmental organization and most recently a human resources intern for a publishing company, I believe I have developed the skills and experience necessary for this role.

To work in human resources, relationship building is essential, a skill which I have acquired through my experience working with people from diverse backgrounds and my naturally outgoing personality. I have also developed good teamwork skills and problem-solving ability which makes me very well suited to this position.

My existing knowledge of this dynamic field coupled with my willingness to learn and adapt to a new working environment mean that I would certainly be a benefit to your company.

[4] I have enclosed my resumé with this letter, which I hope you will take into consideration. Thank you for your time and I look forward to your reply.

[5] Yours sincerely,

Elisa Herbst

Elisa Herbst

Useful phrases for letters of motivation / covering letters

- I am writing to apply ...
- With reference to your advertisement in ... (*newspaper*) of ... (*date*), ...
- ... I would like to applay for the position / post of ...

- I studied ... (*subjects*) at a technical college in ... (*town / city*) from ... (*date*) to ... (*date*).
- I will be finishing school / my education in ...

- As I have always been interested in ..., I would like to get more experience of work in this area before I start work / university.
- I am excited by the possibility of working for your company / organization.
- I would be delighted to be given the chance to work at ...

- I have enclosed my CV / resumé with this letter, which I hope you will take into consideration.
- I enclose a copy of my CV, which shows that I have some experience of dealing with people.
- I have also had the opportunity to take part in several training courses / summer camps.
- As I speak German and English, I would also be able to deal with international visitors / customers.

- Thank you for your time and I look forward to your reply.
- Thank you for considering my application for ...
- I look forward to hearing from you soon.

→ for a model CV, see p. 50

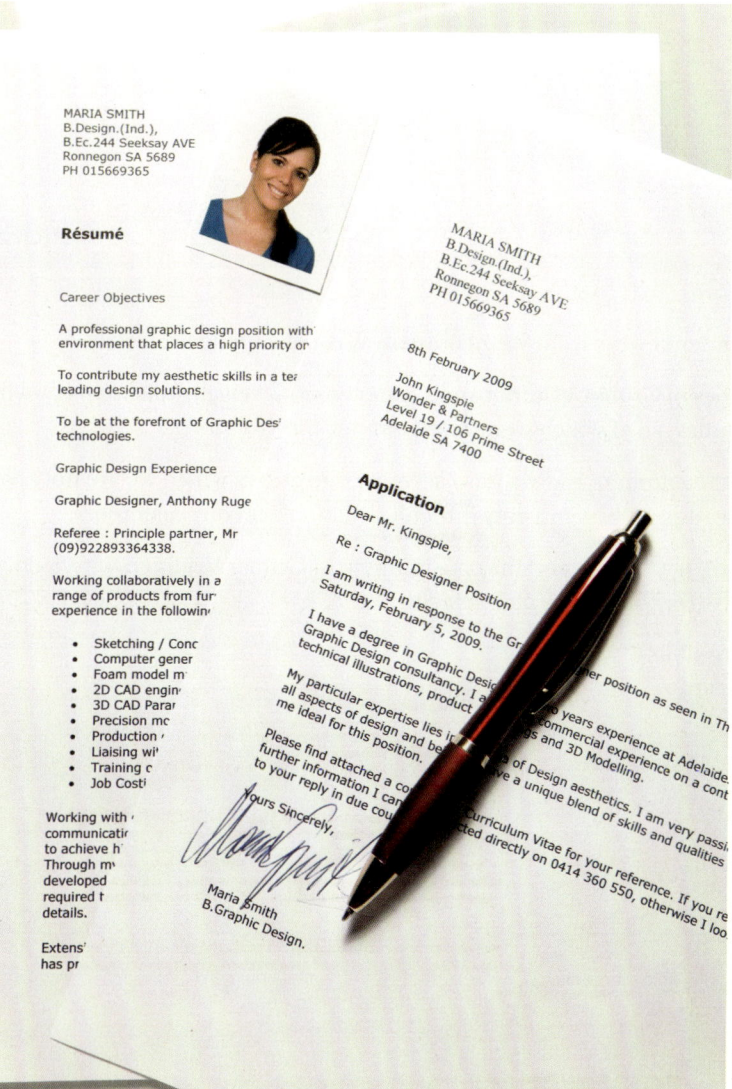

Letter of complaint

Definition	This is a formal letter (or email) addressed to a company or an institution complaining about a product or situation.
Purpose	▪ to inform the company / institution about the situation ▪ to complain about a product / poor service ▪ to request a solution
Target group	the company or institution responsible for the problem
Structure	▪ **Letter:** (company) letterhead; addressee; date; references; subject line [1] ▪ **Email:** addressee; date; subject line ▪ **Salutation:** formal, i.e. *Dear Ms X / Dear Mr Y* or *Dear Sir or Madam* (if you don't have a name) [2] ▪ **Body of the letter / email:** reason for the complaint, giving exact details of order and / or problem; request for action [3] ▪ **Complimentary close;** signature; name and company title, if necessary; enclosure(s); (carbon copies) [4]
Style	▪ formal language

Alimentari Austriaci S.r.l.
Piazza del Popolo
20103 Milano
ITALIA

[1]
Mr Walter Kofler
Weindepot Langenlois GesmbH
Wiener Str. 2
3550 Langenlois
Austria

Order No. 2177344   12 March 20..

[2] Dear Mr Kofler

I am sorry to inform you that the latest order of wine from your company was not supplied correctly.

Our order of 15 February was for 500 bottles of Grüner Veltliner and 500 bottles of Zweigelt. Your delivery, which arrived yesterday, only contained 800 bottles, all of which were Zweigelt.

[3]
Grüner Veltliner is very popular with our customers and we have several large orders which we are not able to fulfil at the moment. As you can imagine, this puts us in a very difficult situation with our customers.

Please let me know as soon as possible when we can expect the consignment of Grüner Veltliner. We would also like to know what we should do with the extra 300 bottles of Zweigelt.

I look forward to your reply as soon as possible.

Yours sincerely

[4]
Vittorio Scilio

Vittorio Scilio
Purchasing Manager

Checklist for letters of complaint

- [ ] Always give the full name and address of the addressee.
- [ ] Give exact details of the order or of the situation you are complaining about.
- [ ] Explain the problem clearly and concisely. Use formal language and always remain polite.
- [ ] Request compensation or a course of action to solve the problem.
- [ ] Use a polite ending and complimentary close.

Useful phrases for letters of complaint

- I am sorry to inform you that our latest order of ... from your company was not supplied correctly / was not to our satisfaction.
- With reference to our order number ... of ... (*date*), I am sorry to have to inform you that some of the items / parts are damaged / broken / missing.

- As you can imagine, this caused us considerable inconvenience.
- This puts us in a very difficult situation with our customers.
- We have a large order from a regular customer, which we have to fill quickly.
- If we do not receive the goods within the next ... days, we will have to stop production.

- Please investigate the matter as soon as possible.
- Please let us know what can be done to solve the problem.
- Please let me know when we can expect the new consignment of ...

- I would like to ask you to ... and to ensure that this does not happen again.
- I am afraid that if these conditions are not met, we may be forced to take legal action.
- We must point out that our further business relationship will depend on a satisfactory solution to this problem.

- I look forward to receiving your explanation of these matters.
- I look forward to your reply as soon as possible.

Enquiry

Definition	This is a formal letter (or email) addressed to a company or institution requesting information about products, services, events, etc.
Purpose	to request information about a product, service or event
Target group	the company or institution responsible for the product, service or event
Structure	■ **Letter:** (company) letterhead; addressee; date; references; subject line ■ **Email:** addressee; date; subject line ■ **Salutation** [1] ■ **Introduction:** subject of the enquiry [2] ■ **Body of the letter / email:** explanation and requests for (specific) information [3] **Conclusion:** request for quick reply [4] ■ **Complimentary close;** signature, name and company title (if necessary) or just name (email) [5]

From: t.michaels@mymail.com
To: info@royalconsulting.com
Subject: Enquiry about Business Controlling Workshop

[1] Dear Sir or Madam

[2] I am writing to enquire whether your institution could offer a course on Business Controlling for our company's Controlling Department.

[3] I checked the course descriptions on your website and decided that the Business Controlling Workshop series (Ref.: BCW 207) might be suitable for us. Especially the focus on European Union project controlling would be of great value to our controlling team, as we are in the process of applying for several EU-funded programs.
I would like to know if it is possible for you to provide a 6-week training course starting at the latest on Thursday, 2 March 20.., for a group of eight people.
Would it be possible for you to send us some more information about the teaching staff and the schedule for this course? In addition, we would be interested in additional workshops and courses related to business and financial controlling in the future.

[4] I am looking forward to your reply.

[5] Kind regards
Thomas Michaels
CEO

Source: Sonja Häusler/Katrin Pürer: Neue Reifeprüfung schriftlich. Englisch BHS. Linz: Veritas 2013, S. 16

Checklist for enquiries

☐ Always give the full name and address of the addressee (letter).

☐ Mention the subject of the enquiry in the subject line.

☐ Explain who you are and why you are interested in the product, service or event.

☐ Clearly request the information you want to know.

☐ Use a polite ending and complimentary close.

Useful phrases for enquiries
- I am writing to enquire whether your institution / company could offer ...
- I would like to know if it is possible (for you) to ...

- We saw your advertisement / brochure / catalogue in ...
- We are a small company / a technical college in ... (*place*) and we are interested in your ... (*product / service*).

- We would like to know if / wheter ...
- Would it be possible for you to send us some more information about ...?
- In addition, we would be interested in :

- We are looking forward to your (early) reply.
- I look forward to hearing from you soon.

Letter to the editor

Definition	This is a letter written by a reader in reply to an article or a column printed in a newspaper or magazine.
Purpose	The reader comments on a particular theme, giving his / her opinion.
Target group	The author of the article or column and the readers of the newspaper / magazine
Structure	■ **Salutation:** *Dear editor* OR: *Sir / Madam* [1] ■ Exact details of the article referred to [2] ■ **Body of the letter:** presentation of arguments, with reasons and examples to back them up [3] ■ **Conclusion:** opinion and summary of arguments [4]; appeal to readers / editor [5] ■ **Close:** name and address [6]
Style	formal language

28 July 20..

[1] Dear editor

[2] I am writing in reply to the article "The internet is a safe place – if you keep your information secret" (Daily Herald, 27 July). In the article, your correspondent argued that internet security was up to individual users. People who posted too much personal information were to blame if they became victims of cybercrimes.

[3] As a matter of fact, these statements were not based on facts because there is a huge amount of information on the internet which we have no control over at all. For example, health records, bank statements and social security details are kept in digital form on computer systems. Any of these systems can be subject to a cyber-attack, no matter how much the institutions invest in security systems.

Secondly, search engines and internet service providers are constantly surveying the websites that we click on to create a profile of who we are. You only need to look at the pop-up ads that appear on the websites you visit to see that "someone out there" knows roughly how old you are, what sex you are and where you live.

[4] People use smartphones to access social networks, send text messages and ring up their friends and / or business colleagues all the time. By doing this, they are just making it easier for government agencies to monitor who they communicate with and what they communicate about.

[5] I call on your newspaper to take the subject of internet security more seriously.

[6] Edward Stone
York

Checklist for letters to the editor

- ☐ Always address the letter to the editor and not to the author of the article.

- ☐ Refer briefly to the information in the article you want to comment on, so that people who have not read the article can easily understand what you want to say.

- ☐ Use formal language, with forceful and effective arguments, but remain polite. Do not try to be funny.

- ☐ Always give your name and address to the editor, even if you want your letter to be published anonymously. Completely anonymous letters are always ignored.

Useful phrases for letters to the editor

- ■ I am writing in reply to the article "... (*name of article*)", in ... (*name of newspaper*), ... (*date*).
- ■ I would like to comment on your article / comment / editorial in the issue of ... (*name of newspaper*), ... (*date*).

- ■ I was sorry / distressed / alarmed to read that ...
- ■ In the article, your correspondent / the author argued / stated that ...
- ■ I am concerned about the way the article ...
- ■ In the article, the author fails to mention ...

- ■ In my opinion, ...
- ■ I (do not) feel / believe / think ...
- ■ I am (totally) opposed to / in favour of ...
- ■ I strongly (dis)agree with ...

- ■ I think it is obvious that ...
- ■ You only need to look at ... to see that ...
- ■ I'm sure that your readers will agree that ...

- ■ I hope my comments / suggestions / points will be taken into consideration.
- ■ I call on your newspaper to ...

3.2 Blog post / comment

Definition	This is a text posted in a blog on the internet, either as an independent entry or as a comment on a previous entry.
Purpose	■ **private:** expressing personal opinions, describing experiences, commenting on previous entries ■ **commercial:** providing customers / business partners with information; advertising / marketing new products; presenting the company image
Target group	■ **private:** friends, family, interested readers ■ **commercial:** customers, employees, business partners
Structure	**Blog post:** ■ title ■ user name ■ date / time ■ introduction ■ body (divided into paragraphs) ■ conclusion **Blog comment:** ■ user name ■ date / time ■ reference to previous entry ■ body (divided into paragraphs) ■ conclusion

---

Where have all the dreamers gone?

Posted by Emelie Hefner

28 July 2018

What is the European Union? Is it just a group of countries that have come together to make their standard of living better or is there more to it than just economics? I started thinking about this on my trip around Europe this summer which happens to coincide with the 100th anniversary of the start of World War I. My trip has taken me through northern France and Belgium, where some of the heaviest fighting took place. Everywhere you go there are cemeteries and memorials to the soldiers who were killed in 1914–18 and 1939–45.

Some people think that the European Union has too much power, is too bureaucratic and costs too much. But anyone who has seen the cemeteries in Verdun or on the Somme knows that it is much more important than that. The countries of the European Union have been at peace with each other since 1945, something that would not have been possible a few generations ago.

Now Europeans can travel without borders and trade with each other without customs taxes. We can get to know other cultures and countries first-hand. We all, well, almost all of us, use the same currency.

So, I say to all the Eurosceptics and Euro-critics out there: take a trip to some of the battlefields of Flanders and think about what the alternative to the European Union might be. It is not perfect; it might cost a lot of money, but I think it is a price worth paying. What about you?

Checklist for blog posts / comments

☐ Always give your (user) name and date.

☐ If you are commenting on a blog post, refer to the information, ideas or arguments in that post.

☐ Use informal, conversational language for a private blog; a commercial blog may be more neutral. Contractions (*I'm, can't*, etc.) are allowed in both.

☐ You can be funny, depending on the subject you are dealing with.

☐ You can address your readers directly and ask them to post comments with their own ideas and opinions.

3.3 Report

Definition	The presentation of a particular situation in the form of a(n official) document; based on information from an investigation by an appointed person or group of people.
Purpose	To inform the reader about the situation, to draw conclusions and / or to make recommendations.
Target group	A person, or persons, of authority, either in a company or an institution.
Structure	■ Addressee(s) [1] ■ Author(s) [2] ■ Subject [3] ■ Date [4] ■ Paragraphs (usually with subheadings) [5] ■ Conclusion and / or recommendations [6]

Division of household tasks: by gender, Great Britain

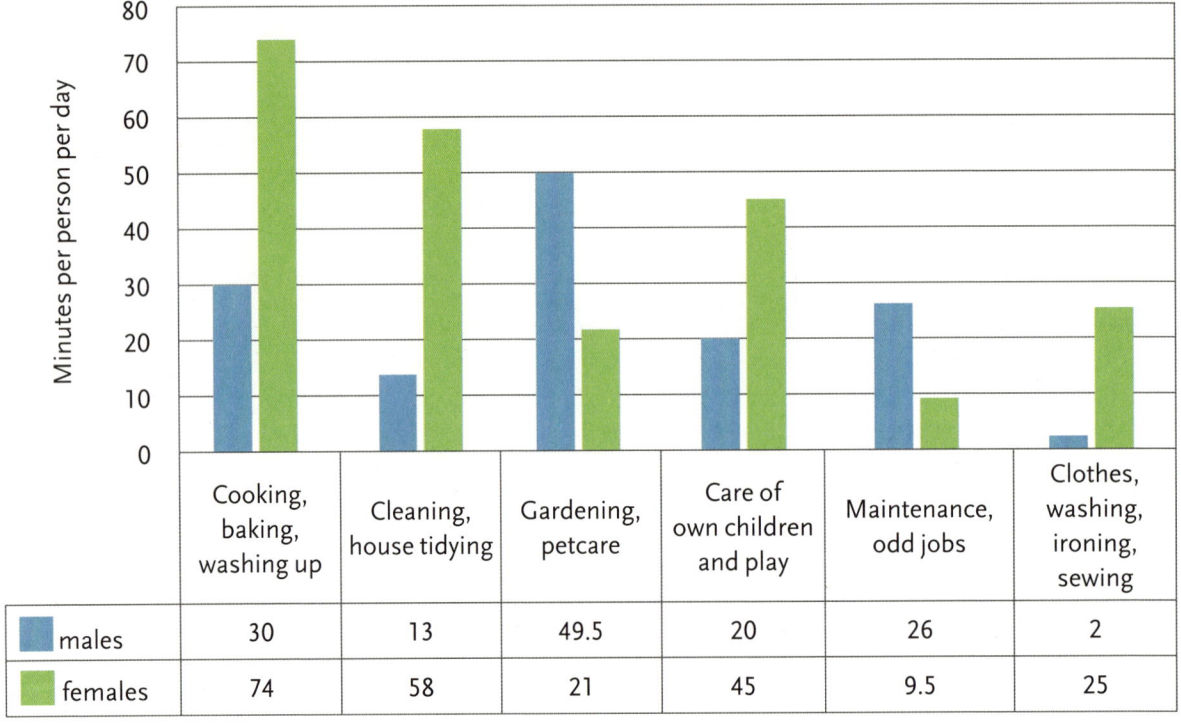

	Cooking, baking, washing up	Cleaning, house tidying	Gardening, petcare	Care of own children and play	Maintenance, odd jobs	Clothes, washing, ironing, sewing
males	30	13	49.5	20	26	2
females	74	58	21	45	9.5	25

[1] To: Mr. Hubert
[2] From: Melanie Talent
[4] Date: 31.01.20..

[3] **Subject: Analysis of household tasks done by men and women in Great Britain.**

Introduction
The chart above provides an overview of the average amount of time British men and women use for domestic tasks. In general, it can be seen that women spend four hours on household tasks, while men only spend approximately two and a half hours.

Household tasks performed by women and men
[5] According to the chart, women are more likely to perform tasks connected to cooking, cleaning, washing and childcare. In comparison, women spend about 74 minutes on cooking, baking and washing up, while men only spend 30 minutes in doing these tasks. In addition, women use 58 minutes a day for tasks such as cleaning and house tidying, whereas men devote just 13 minutes to these activities. However, there are a few areas where men are more active than women, i.e. gardening, pet care and maintenance jobs around the house. The statistics say that men spend 49.5 minutes a day on gardening and pet care, while women spend only 21 minutes in doing these tasks.

Recommendation
To achieve a balance, it is recommended to initiate measures concerning equal distribution of household chores. This can be achieved through an extensive advertising campaign including television, radio and newspapers.

Conclusion
[6] All in all, the chart above underlines the fact that routine domestic duties are primarily taken care of by women, while men prefer tasks like gardening, house maintenance and pet care.

Source: Sonja Häusler / Karin Pürer: Neue Reifeprüfung schriftlich. Englisch AHS. Linz: Veritas 2015, S. 17

Checklist for reports

- ☐ Always give the addressee, the author's name and the subject of the report.

- ☐ Analyse any statistics or diagrams as clearly and precisely as possible.

- ☐ Draw conclusions from the statistics and make sensible and suitable recommendations.

- ☐ Use sub-headings to show clearly what each paragraph is about.

- ☐ Use formal or neutral language. Do not use contractions: I am (not ~~I'm~~), We cannot (not ~~we can't~~)

Useful phrases for reports
- The aim of this report is to ...
- The chart above provides an overview of ...
- The chart above shows (how many) ...
- In general, it can be seen that ..., while ...

- According to the chart, ...
- In addition, ...
- In comparison, ...
- However, ...
- The statistics say that ...

- (To improve this situation,) I would suggest / recommend that ...
- This can be achieved through ...
- We should / could also consider ...

- All in all, the chart above underlines the fact that ..., while ...

3.4 Article

Definition	An article is a written text on a particular theme that is a separate part of a larger online or printed publication, such as a book, magazine or newspaper.
Purpose	▪ To inform the reader in a neutral way. ▪ Depending on the nature of the publication, an article can also be used to entertain, to persuade or to provoke a reaction.
Target group	An article is directed at the readers of a particular publication. The type of publication is always given in the task instructions.
Structure	▪ **Title**, or **headline** and subheadline; often a play on words [1] ▪ **Introduction:** a lead-in that attracts the readers' interest [2] ▪ **Body** of the article: divided into paragraphs for each main point; ideas and different aspects can be supported by dates and facts, if appropriate [3] ▪ **Conclusion:** demonstrating the purpose of the article – is it meant to inform, provoke or interest the reader? [4]

[1] **Virtual reality: better than the real thing?**

[2] What do you do when your life is grey and uninteresting or your job is so boring that you need something exciting to look forward to at the weekend? Answer: Dress up as Darth Vader and go to the Vienna Comix Convention!

[3] That's exactly what I did last weekend – well, without the dressing-up, actually, but that was a big mistake, as the visitors who weren't in costume were a very small minority. And all the people in character looked at me as if I was the strange one! There were people in custumes everywhere, from Elves, Dwarfs and Orcs to Klingons and Princess Leila. And they all looked great!

Although I looked a bit out of place, I did feel slightly superior to all those people dressed as fantasy and comic characters: I mean, don't they have anything better to do than dress up at the weekend? Are their lives so boring that they need to escape?

But then my journalistic training got the better of me and I started asking a few of the visitors why they were there. The most common answers were: "to have fun", "to meet friends or interesting people", "to find out about new trends in the world of fantasy". It seemed that everybody was just out to enjoy themselves. I started to feel that I was slightly strange because I couldn't seem to enjoy the day for what it was: good entertainment.

Nobody said they were there because their life was so boring, or their job so tedious. These were perfectly normal people with perfectly normal jobs. I spoke to a bus driver, two nurses, a baker, a policeman, even a doctor (Darth Vader) and a lawyer (Princess Leila). They were all people with busy, demanding, fulfilling jobs. I suspect that changing character for the weekend is a good way to take your mind off chasing criminals or fighting cancer.

[4] So next time I see an advert for the Vienna Comix Convention, what am I going to do? Get dressed up and go and join the fun, of course! See you there …

Checklist for articles

- ☐ Read the instructions carefully. Make sure you know exactly what the topic of the article should be.
- ☐ Make sure that you understand the nature of the publication and the target audience.
- ☐ Collect ideas and put them in a logical order.
- ☐ Think about what the main message of the article should be. Use this in your conclusion.
- ☐ Use formal or informal language, depending on the nature of your target audience.

Useful words and phrases: → see p. 46, Linking ideas

3.5 Leaflet / brochure

Definition and purpose	Leaflets and brochures are often used as advertising material. They are written to convince the reader of a certain product or service.
Target group	The target group depends on the purpose of the leaflet or brochure (= the specific task), e.g. if it is aimed at potential or at regular customers.
Structure / Layout	■ Find a **catchy headline or title.** [1] ■ **Introduction:** state what the leaflet is about. (What is being advertised?) [2] ■ **Main part:** the most relevant information is given in short, concise form. [3] Use paragraphs with headlines [4] and / or bullet points. Say why the product / service is special / helpful, etc. ■ **End** with a summary of the main points and ask for action – e.g. to donate or buy sth – and provide contact details. [5]
Style	Persuasive language; language of advertising
Tip	Include attractive pictures and, if appropriate, statistics to present the information in an interesting way.

[1] **GREAT ASIAN FOOD – DELIVERED TO YOUR DOOR**

[2] *ExpressAsia is the best and fastest Asian food delivery service for the whole of London.*

[3 + 4] **The very best Asian food:**
ExpressAsia offers a huge choice of 365 different Asian specialities – one for each day of the year! On our menu you will find Thai, Indian, Chinese, Japanese and Vietnamese dishes. The list is endless. ExpressAsia has been voted the best food delivery service in London. Our chefs are working constantly to bring you the very best of Asian cooking.

Quick and easy:
Our express delivery service guarantees a hot meal delivered to your door within 45 minutes of your order. All you need is one telephone call, text message or email to make your order. We do the rest while you enjoy your evening.

NEW ExpressAsia app:
You are on your way home from work? You don't know what to eat? With the new ExpressAsia app you can order direct from your smartphone. If you open an ExpressAsia personal account, you can follow your order online, write reviews of the dishes and pay for your orders at the end of the month. Account holders also get free delivery for orders over £25.

[5] Open your personal account now to get the best of Asian cooking delivered free to your home.
Visit www.expressasia.co.uk for more details or to download our menu.

Westway, London W2 9JP. Tel: 023 924678. Email: office@expressasia.co.uk

Checklist for leaflets

- ☐ Make sure the headline tells the reader what is being advertised.
- ☐ The first paragraph contains all basic necessary information.
- ☐ The other paragraphs provide additional information.
- ☐ Use adjectives for describing your product and avoid negations.
- ☐ Include information about the company and contact details.

4   Language for tasks ("Operatoren")

The instructions say:	What is expected:
advise [əd'vaɪz] *(also:* **give (sb.) advice on***)*	Tell somebody what you think they should do in a particular situation. ('beraten') *Give them some advice on how to improve their marks.* ▶ recommend, suggest
analyse *(BE),* **analyze** *(AE)* ['ænəlaɪz]	Look at something in detail and explain its meaning and / or structure. ('analysieren') *Analyse the main elements of the poster.* ▶ examine
apologize [ə'pɒlədʒaɪz]	Say that you are sorry for doing something wrong or causing a problem. ('sich entschuldigen') *Apologize for the delay in delivery.*
argue ['ɑːgjuː] *(also:* **give arguments***)*	Give reasons why you think that something is right / wrong, true / not true, etc., especially to persuade people that you are right. ('begründen, erörtern') *Give arguments for and against globalization.* ▶ give reasons
ask	Tell somebody that you would like them to do something or that you would like something to happen; or that you would like somebody to give you something. ('fragen, darum bitten') *Ask for the goods to be delivered as soon as possible.*
comment on ['kɒment]	Express your opinion on something, giving evidence to support your view. ('kommentieren') *Comment on the speaker's belief that ...*
compare	Explain similarities and differences between two or more things. ('vergleichen') *Compare how the characters are portrayed in the film and in the novel.*
complain *(also:* **make a complaint***)*	Say that you are annoyed, unhappy or not satisfied about somebody / something. ('sich beschweren') *Write a letter of complaint to the manufacturer of the faulty goods.*
consider [kən'sɪdə(r)]	Think about something carefully, especially in order to make a decision. ('erwägen, in Betracht ziehen') *Consider the different views of individual freedom around the world.* ▶ evaluate
contrast [kən'trɑːst]	Show the differences between two or more things. ('kontrastieren') *Contrast the rights of African Americans in the 1960s and today.*
convince [kən'vɪns]	Make somebody believe that something is true; or persuade somebody to do something. ('überzeugen') *Try to convince your partner that your suggestion will work.* ▶ persuade
demonstrate ['demənstreɪt]	Show something clearly by giving proof or evidence. ('beweisen, darlegen') *Demonstrate the connection between junk food and obesity.*
describe *(also:* **give / write a description of***)*	State what something or somebody is like, including all the relevant details. ('beschreiben') *Describe the writer's invention and what it is used for.*
discuss	Look carefully at something from all sides before stating your opinion. It should be clear from what has gone before, how and why you arrived at this opinion. ('diskutieren, erörtern') *Discuss how education influences attitudes towards immigration.*
emphasize ['emfəsaɪz]	Give special importance to something. ('hervorheben') *Give reasons for the decline of newspapers, emphasizing the role of digital media.*

The instructions say:	What is expected:
encourage [ɪnˈkʌrɪdʒ]	Persuade somebody to do something by making it easier for them and making them believe it is a good thing to do. ('ermutigen, ermuntern') *Explain the benefits of healthy eating and encourage them to take regular exercise.*
evaluate [ɪˈvæljueɪt]	Show the pros and cons of something in a balanced way, and then give an opinion on it. ('einschätzen, bewerten') *Evaluate the author's view of the impact King's speech had on his audience.* ▶ consider
examine [ɪgˈzæmɪn]	Look at something in detail and explain its meaning and / or structure. ('untersuchen, prüfen') *Examine the writer's attitude towards the protagonist.* ▶ analyse
exemplify [ɪgˈzemplɪfaɪ] *(also:* **give (an) example(s) of**)	Give an example in order to make something clearer. ('erläutern, veranschaulichen') *Point out the effects of smoking on health, giving examples.*
explain	State what something is like and give reasons why it is that way. ('erklären') *Explain the main character's reaction to her mother in the first scene.*
give an / your opinion	Say your feelings or thoughts about somebody / something. ('Meinung äußern') *Give you opinion of the author's view as expressed in her blog entry.*
give reasons	Give an explanation for something. ('beweisen, darlegen') *State your opinion of the topic, giving reasons.* ▶ argue
inform [ɪnˈfɔːm]	Tell somebody about something, especially in an official way. ('benachrichtigen') *Inform the customer that the delivery has been delayed.*
instruct [ɪnˈstrʌkt] *(also:* **give instructions**)	Tell somebody to do something, especially in a formal or an official way; or give somebody information about something. ('in Kenntnis setzen, anweisen') *Give the new colleague instructions on how to use the photocopier.*
introduce [ˌɪntrəˈdjuːs]	Present something or somebody new. ('einführen, vorstellen') *Introduce the visitors to the company to your boss.*
offer	Say that you are willing to do something for somebody or give something to somebody. ('anbieten, einen Vorschlag unterbreiten') *Offer to replace the damaged goods at your expense.*
outline	State the main features and structure of a text. ('umreißen, skizzieren') *Outline the writer's views on …*
persuade [pəˈsweɪd]	Make somebody do something by giving them good reasons for doing it. ('überzeugen') *Try to persuade your colleagues to work with the new computer program.* ▶ convince
point out	Identify something and present it clearly. ('benennen, darlegen') *Point out the keywords in the first paragraph of the text.*
present [prɪˈzent]	(Re)structure something and write it down. ('darstellen') *Present your ideas in a logical order.*
recommend [ˌrekəˈmend] *(also:* **make recommendations**)	Advise somebody to do something; or tell somebody that something is good or useful, or that somebody would be suitable for a particular job, etc. ('empfehlen, befürworten') *Make recommendations on how to improve the situation.* ▶ advise, suggest
report *(also:* write a report)	Give people information about something that you have heard, seen, done, etc. ('berichten') *Write a report, giving details of the survey results.* ▶ say

The instructions say:	What is expected:
say	Give people information about something that you have heard, seen, done, etc. ('berichten') *Give your opinion of the program, saying whether you would like to use it .* ▶ report
specify ['spesɪfaɪ]	State something clearly, by giving exact details. ('darlegen') *Specify the reasons for the delay in delivery.* ▶ state
speculate ['spekjuleɪt]	Form and express an opinion about something even if you don't know all the details or facts. ('mutmaßen, Vermutungen anstellen') *Speculate on reasons why the company is so successful.*
state	Specify something clearly. ('darlegen') *State your opinion on the main character's decision.*
suggest [sə'dʒest]	Put forward an idea or a plan for other people to think about. ('vorschlagen, empfehlen') *Suggest ways in which international co-operation could be improved.* ▶ advise, recommend
summarize *(also:* **give / write a summary of; sum up***)*	Present the main points of something in a short and clear form, leaving out details and examples. ('zusammenfassen') *Summarize the incident in the church in no more than four sentences.*